Exotic Panzers in Miniature

Exotic Panzers in Miniature

Modeling Unusual War Machines of the Third Reich

Edward F. McGrane

Schiffer Military History
Atglen, PA

Dedication

For Matt Reinert
A gentleman and a scholar, but not necessarily in that order.

The illustrations included in this book, as well as many others are available for purchase from the author. Please contact the author through Schiffer Publishing for further details.

Book Design by Ian Robertson.

Library of Congress Catalog Number: 2001095302

Printed in China.
ISBN: 0-7643-1469-6

We are interested in hearing from authors with book ideas on related topics.

Published by Schiffer Publishing Ltd.
4880 Lower Valley Road
Atglen, PA 19310
Phone: (610) 593-1777
FAX: (610) 593-2002
E-mail: Schifferbk@aol.com.
Visit our web site at: www.schifferbooks.com
Please write for a free catalog.
This book may be purchased from the publisher.
Please include $3.95 postage.
Try your bookstore first.

In Europe, Schiffer books are distributed by:
Bushwood Books
6 Marksbury Avenue
Kew Gardens
Surrey TW9 4JF
England
Phone: 44 (0) 20 8392-8585
FAX: 44 (0) 20 8392-9876
E-mail: Bushwd@aol.com.
Free postage in the UK. Europe: air mail at cost.
Try your bookstore first.

Contents

Foreword

"TRUTH IS MORE THAN REALITY," author Paul Carell wrote in his esteemed book *Operation Barbarossa in Photographs*. At first glance this stark statement appears to be a tautology. What, after all, is the difference between truth and reality? And further, what is the significance of Mr. Carell's proposition to the art of modeling miniature armored fighting vehicles (AFVs), figures, and terrain base settings?

Here, I do not employ the word "art" loosely. To be sure, the majority of model builders continue to regard our pursuit as an outlet for relaxation, a more or less casual diversion. But just as surely, sculptors and painters of military miniatures have in only the last thirty years or so elevated this craft to a fine art form. For these modelers—the comparative few—there is no turning back; for them, miniature making is a labor of love, and they chase after their passion with the same fervor as any portrait artist, musician, animator, or architect.

To return to the question, though—truth is indeed more than reality. Truth, the stuff of art, is that which endures, that which carries an independent significance no matter what the context. Reality is merely the momentary state of things, existence conditioned by circumstances. Military miniature artists, like all artists, are concerned not only with fidelity to time, or to place, or to scale details, but with the broad truths of their chosen subject: the human experience of warfare.

The extremes of the human experience come into focus during war. Indeed, as any veteran can tell you, war is, if anything, a heightened experience. Where else is heroism so readily apparent, cowardice so hard to miss? Where else are life and death such intimate confrères? The history of war is an ongoing chronicle of the best and worst moments of the human condition. To one degree or another, military miniature art tries to faithfully capture these moments. As with all art forms, it aims to provide a glimpse of the human condition. At its best, it is a glimpse that strikes a chord deep within the spectator, whether he sees it from the vantage point of the miniaturist or of the layman. Whatever the chosen subject, and however accurately that subject has been captured, a work of miniature art simply rings true.

A Truly Exotic Panzer: The hypothetical E-10 tank destroyer. This 1/35 scale model, produced by the resin kit manufacturer **Cromwell** of Scotland, is based upon German drawing board designs from later in the Second World War. The actual vehicle never saw service. "But what if it had?" is the question fans of German AFVs perennially pose. This book advances at least a partial answer to that question, through the medium of military miniature art.

In Command: The E-10's gritty, vigorous "captain."

Exotic Panzers

My enthusiasm for modeling armored fighting vehicles (AFVs) started at age ten. Today, after twenty-eight years, it goes on unabated. During that time I have built quite a few plastic model kits. However, with my latest efforts I have tried to bring to my work a respect for the artistic truth of which Mr. Carell speaks. These, my most recent projects, form the collection of military miniatures presented in these pages.

What follows is a series of photographic essays, each dealing with a diorama or vignette centered upon an exotic panzer. By "exotic panzer" I refer to a little-known or entirely hypothetical tank, assault gun, or other vehicle of the German ground forces of the Second World War. Common to most of these panzers is that they have had limited coverage in historical or modeling books, magazines, or documentaries. Some represent educated guesses at possible modifications, innovations that could have been introduced by soldiers in the field; others are derived strictly from the drawing board, and are based upon vehicles that were never actually produced, or which saw only abbreviated service during the war.

I have made a case for trying to incorporate the truths of human experience into the process of creating military miniatures. Without reservation, I have maintained that modeling the human experience of war is an artistic pursuit. Why, then, have I chosen to model exotic panzers? By "exotic," am I not describing a rarity, something far removed from the ordinary? Indeed, would not ordinary, well-documented subjects better lend themselves to projects that highlight the human experience?

In answer, I must first confess a total and long-abiding fascination with all of the German panzers. To me, the German tank armies were to World War Two what Hannibal's formations were to the Punic Wars, or what Robert E. Lee's Army of Northern Virginia was to the War Between the States (or American Civil War). They were the underdogs, but in their situation, brilliant underdogs—vanquished not because of ineptitude or cowardice, but because of political events and economic realities which they themselves could hardly have hoped to influence. I think a good number of armor enthusiasts model German subjects not only for their peculiar charisma, but because they share this admiration of the underdog. And while many of us have given over fair time to the study of the armor of the other belligerents of the Second World War, the German panzers continue to hold a particular appeal for us. I suspect that they will exert their lure for as long as there are armor enthusiasts.

The Machine and the Land are One: The E-10 tears across a stretch of soggy, fallow grass beside the bank of a shallow stream. By putting the subject in a realistic environment (here, early winter, 1946), it becomes far more than simply a scale representation. It becomes part of an event, the subject of an "historical snapshot."

Human Resources: Well-executed AFV dioramas and vignettes successfully integrate human figures with vehicular and environmental elements. Note the broad distance between the tops of the wheels and the hull overhang (sponson) on this compact tank hunter. Designed to lie in wait and ambush the enemy from concealed positions, the E-10 was to be specially fitted with an hydraulic suspension that would allow its hull to drop onto the track runs, giving it an extremely low profile.

After building models of most of the "classic" (i.e., commonly employed) panzers, it was inevitable that the rare topics, the exceptions to the rule—the *exotic* panzers—would sooner or later grab my attention. However, if I ever thought that switching my focus to obscure or hypothetical vehicles would liberate me from the constraints of realism and technical accuracy, I did not think so for long. To the contrary, I was to learn that exotic panzers demand even more cautious and considered study than do the classic panzers, and can pose even greater challenges to one's imagination. The classic panzers, with their wealth of supporting source materials, can be built to occupy any kind of diorama or vignette; an exotic panzer tends to call for a scene wherein the time and place are specified. Moreover, there is usually an absence of substantial source materials covering the exotic panzer. It therefore becomes even more the portion of the modeler to envision and execute a believable setting for it.

This, however, is where the immense satisfaction begins, because the new perspective that has to be taken while modeling an exotic panzer is a welcome one. It is a perspective that relies less upon what *must* have been and more upon *what might very possibly have been*. Although there are always standards of technical and historical realism to observe, these are not so restrictive with exotic panzers as they are with the classic panzers.

To illustrate, consider one of the truly classic panzers, the Pz.Kpfw. VI Tiger. If you were to build a Tiger tank assigned to the 501st Heavy Panzer Battalion in Tunisia in 1943, your research would show that tanks in that battalion at that time were fitted with non-standard exhaust covers and front fenders, and that the headlights were mounted in an unusual manner. To build a realistic representation of this early Tiger, you would have to make sure your model featured these distinct design departures. I do not mean to say in any way that this would be an exercise in drudgery; to the contrary, it is entirely satisfying—and as much of an artistic venture—to modify an AFV kit to fit a well-documented scene.

Exotic panzers, however, make wholly different research demands of the modeler. Consider the model of the hypothetical E-10 tank destroyer, the exotic panzer pictured throughout this foreword. Although it is a fine resin kit from **Cromwell** of Scotland, it comes with few surface details, probably because it was patterned after a blueprint. Because I wanted to model mine as it might have appeared in service, I had to determine where to place tools, extra gear, and common German AFV fixtures, such as attachment points for jerry cans. Following my intuition, I added a more intricate exhaust system than was supplied. Further, choices had to be made for the color scheme, and for any tactical markings. This process was quite different from the one I would use with the early Tiger, or for that matter any classic panzer. Truly, it called for speculation—educated speculation.

"Please Pardon Our Appearance": Mud and rust effects on the rear armor of the E-10. With AFV dioramas and vignettes, the terrain modeling possibilities are limitless, but the challenge of effectively uniting a subject with its environment can intimidate. The project essays of this book cover a broad variety of terrain types, as well as vehicle soiling and damage. Each essay describes the specific modeling techniques used to simulate both terrain and vehicle "weathering."

Articles of War: Most of the on-board equipment seen in this picture did not come with the E-10 kit. The towing clevis, chain, fire extinguisher, and wire cutters came from other AFV kits or accessory sets. The wire strands crossing each other to the left of the clevis would hold branches and foliage for camouflage.

Which brings us back to the beginning, Mr. Carell's observation that truth is greater than reality. Indeed, as with any historical miniature subject, modeling an exotic panzer requires attention to realism and accuracy. But as we have seen, even more is required. Since exotic panzers so rarely come with historical source materials, educated speculation becomes all the more important. And it seems to me that this is best assisted by resorting to a guiding principle that has served artists of all disciplines so well for centuries: *bring truth to your subject.*

Edward F. McGrane
April, 2001

A Truly Exotic Panzer

From Conception to Completion: Heavy Tank Destroyer "Zerstörer"

SOMETIME IN 1943, A PROPOSAL FOR A HEAVY TANK destroyer made its way to the drawing boards of the German Armaments Ministry. Designated the 12.8 cm L/55 auf Pz.Kpfw. V Zerstörer (or "Destroyer"), the project was considered only briefly, then shelved because the design was thought to be unfeasible.

Ultimately, the monster 12.8 cm gun would find its home on a modified Pz.Kpfw. VI Tiger II chassis as the business end of the classic Jagdtiger, the heaviest tank destroyer to see action during the Second World War.

However improbable it may have been to hope to marry the huge 12.8 cm L/55 to the Panther's medium-weight chassis and power plant, the proposed Zerstörer design is still intriguing. Borrowing heavily from the Panther for its sleek angles and crowned in the rear by a curiously boxy fighting compartment, it would have made a truly impressive prototype.

Hobbymodellbau of Germany no doubt agreed about the Zerstörer's peculiar charisma when they produced it as a resin conversion kit. Intended for use with **Tamiya's** late Panther G, steel-wheeled version, this conversion is as rare as its subject is exotic. When I found the kit on a vendor's table at a miniatures show, I knew instantly that I had to buy it. In my view, the Zerstörer is the ultimate exotic panzer—mythical, majestic, menacing.

The essay that follows covers the assembly, detailing, and finishing of the Zerstörer. Techniques for working with resin conversion parts and fabricating a partial vehicle interior are discussed, as are approaches to making educated super-detailing choices for "drawing-board panzers."

12.8 cm Pak 44 L/55 Zerstörer auf Panther F.

Mind and Matter: A variety of references furnished the inspiration for the planning, construction, and super-detailing of the Zerstörer *(upper left)*. Although the actual Zerstörer never made it past the drawing board, in production it would have borrowed components from the Panther and Tiger II series of vehicles, so books on those subjects provided valuable insight for making the Zerstörer into miniature reality. Besides the **Hobbymodellbau** resin conversion kit (*yellow box top, lower left*), **Dragon's** Panther F and Jagdtiger (Henschel) kits supplied key parts for the project.

. . .And You Were There: In this close-up of the right-rear quarter of the Grille, the perforated muffler shield appears delicate in comparison with the armor plating of the rest of the vehicle. "Soldier's-eye views" like this are often more instructive to the miniaturist than schematics and contemporary photos.

Assembly Notes: After-market Accessories and Tools

Mail Order Magic: After-market AFV kit accessories range in price and scope from inexpensive styrene bolts and rivets to comprehensive super-detailing sets that often cost more than the kits for which they are designed.
The use of some after-market products is practically a given when building exotic panzers, and instances of their use are highlighted throughout this book. The items shown at right—lathed aluminum gun barrels, photo-etch brass, and the like—are usually not found in mainstream hobby shops, but must be ordered from cottage industries or large hobby distributors.

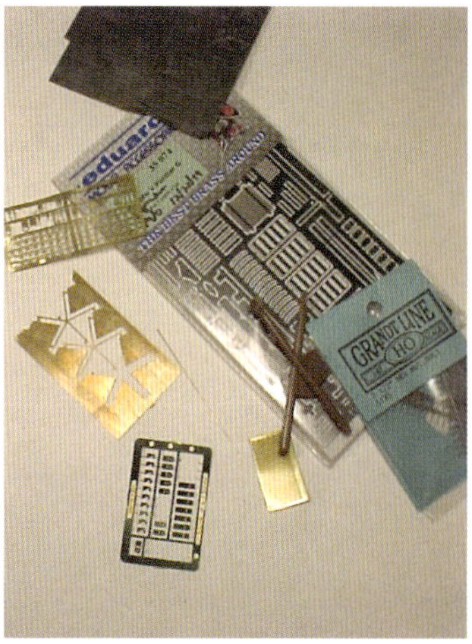

Up-Close and Personal: Ordnance museums are equally valuable for reference, and are certainly inspirational to the armor enthusiast who is fortunate enough to live close to one. The museum at Aberdeen Proving Ground, Maryland, boasts one of the most comprehensive collections of armor in the world, and includes relatively rare vehicles like the German Grille M self-propelled howitzer *(above)*.
Seeing a real AFV in person is quite a revelation. Particularly noteworthy is the great variation in the metal thickness of the vehicle's components. When compared against the heavy armor plating of the gun mantlet, lighter features, such as the fenders and equipment clasps, seem paper-thin—as if designed to be easily torn away in a scrape. Such observations are enormously helpful, even when researching a drawing-board AFV like the Zerstörer.

A Word to the Wise: Although not aggressively marketed to the general kit-building hobby public, after-market has become *big* business. Almost everything imaginable for use with AFV kits has been produced by someone. The challenge, then, is not in finding useful parts and accessories, but in making those purchasing choices that will most enhance your modeling experience without breaking your bank.
That said, shopping for after-market accessories can be one of the most enjoyable aspects of building a miniature AFV. If you're like me, you will happily look forward to those mail order boxes of accessories at your door.

Generic Brands: The items shown above are generally useful for super-detailing AFV projects; all of these materials seem to find their way into each of mine. Pictured are copper and brass sheets; aluminum and lead foils; fine brass rods; plastic tubing; various gauges of metal wire; electrical solder; and thread for model ship rigging. These can be found at hobby and hardware stores.
The container at upper left holds an assortment of potentially useful odds and ends, and the film canister at upper right contains baking soda powder. When sprinkled onto wet hobby paint, baking soda effectively simulates ground-in dirt on vehicle surfaces, and imparts corroded textures to mufflers and exhaust pipes.

Assembly Notes, Continued: An Exotic Panzer is Born

Genesis: The basic components of the Zerstörer, laid out on the worktable for an initial test-fit. The hull is from the styrene Dragon Panther F kit. The superstructure from the Hobbymodellbau conversion kit, though almost identical in color, is actually a resin casting. Tan and cream-colored resin are far more common to after-market kits.

My construction and super-detailing tools range from costly but time-saving styrene sprue nippers to cheap household disposables, such as emery boards, toothbrushes, and toothpicks. These last are for one-time use when applying glues and putties. Other tools include a small metal ruler and jeweler's files.

Discussion: Your tool assortment will evolve as your construction techniques broaden. For example, some years ago I struck upon using a soldering iron with a file-sharpened tip to burn "welding scars" into the armor plate joints of plastic AFV kits. Be open to experimentation, and keep an eye out for tools that look like they may improve upon a technique, or at least help you work more efficiently.

Let There Not Be Light: White styrene sheet was cut to fit and glued to the inside of the forward hull top, against the two rectangular engine grill openings. When the model is finished, these styrene shims will block the empty forward interior from view. The shims will be sprayed with the dark brown base color to suggest a dark interior underneath the photo-etch grills.

Why Resin?

Resin is the medium of choice for the after-market makers of accessories, conversion sets, and even whole AFV kits. Although resin itself is relatively inexpensive, the casting process is labor-intensive, and is as much an art as it is a science. But the best resin kits boast a fidelity to scale detail that many styrene kit manufacturers still find impractical or altogether impossible to achieve.

A trade-off for this increased detail is the extra care required when preparing and assembling resin. While the best styrene kits present their parts on durable, well-engineered sprues, resin kits typically come in just a few large pieces, each having an unwieldy "plug" of resin overpour that must be shaved away with extreme caution. The smaller details can be delicate enough to arrive warped or even broken in the box, and the parts that do make it to the worktable intact can easily be broken during kit construction. *Lastly (and most importantly), the act of sanding and scraping resin creates a toxic dust, so a respirator or at least a dust mask should always be worn while working with resin parts.*

These quirks notwithstanding, resin kits carry a special appeal, mainly because their manufacturers concentrate on elusive subjects as yet unavailable in styrene. Not surprisingly, the exotic panzers featured in this book are mostly resin kits, and some of them may never be available in styrene. Furthermore, there is a distinct satisfaction in rising to the challenges posed by constructing resin subjects. Hopefully, the techniques described in this essay will prove helpful to those readers who are new to this medium.

I chose Dragon's Panther F styrene kit as the basis for the Zerstörer project. Because the Hobbymodellbau conversion was not designed for this kit, I had to make a few adjustments during assembly. One was to fashion sheet styrene sponsons (the plates below the superstructure overhang that run above the tops of the tracks). This required some trial-and-error cutting and fitting to make the sponsons fit both the rough interior of the resin superstructure and the lower hull of the Dragon kit.

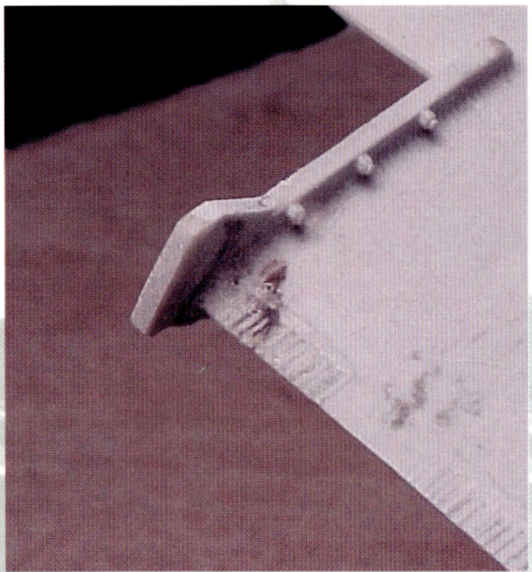

The edges and contours of even the largest resin kit parts can be fragile. My Zerstörer's superstructure came with a chipped tow shackle mount. Unable to find the broken piece in the box, I had to restore it by sculpting a new one with **A+B** epoxy putty, copying from the mount on the opposite side.

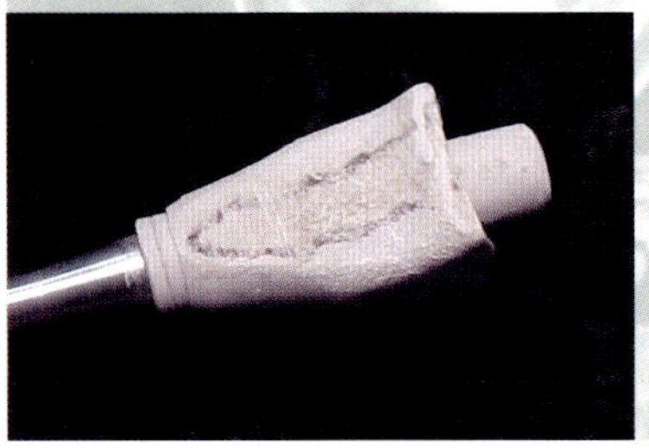

A similar correction had to be made to an irregular recess on the bottom of the gun mantlet. The defective area, here outlined in pencil, was easily filled with epoxy putty and stippled with a toothbrush to restore its cast metal texture.

Excitement by Repetition: The construction of the suspension and running gear is usually the first assembly step of an AFV kit's instructions. Even when it isn't, I make it a point to tackle this step first. With numerous identical parts comprising the road wheels, return rollers, and link-to-link tracks, there is tedium in the preparation, so it's best to get this step out of the way early. Like the light, repetitive exercises of a sprinter, the building of the running gear makes a good warm-up for breaking into the rest of the work.

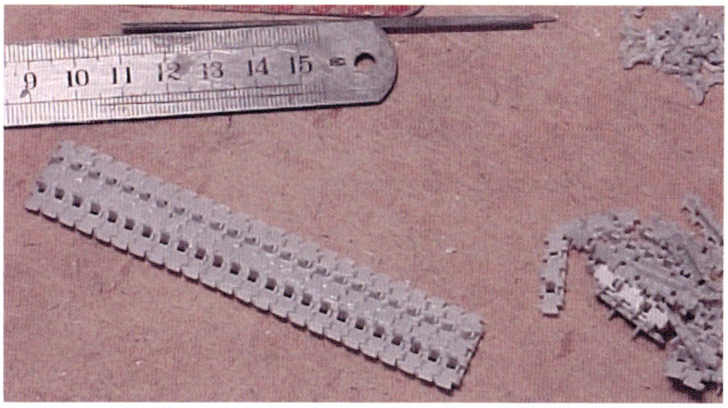

As is common to so many of the newer styrene AFV kits, the Dragon Panther F tracks come as individual links. Although their assembly requires much repetitious clean-up, they present the modeler with the opportunity to create truly realistic track runs. Real AFV tracks are weighty, tending to sag along their upper runs in the gaps between road wheels and return rollers. This effect is more or less pronounced, depending upon how the track tension has been adjusted and the number of links present in the runs. In the picture above, one of the track runs is being assembled. As with the road wheels, a metal straight-edge helps to keep the individual links properly aligned.

Though more convenient to assemble, the single-piece vinyl tracks of older AFV kits are much more difficult to fix in place so as to simulate the weighty properties of real track links. The extra work required to make them behave like the prototype is seldom worth your while. You may prefer instead to invest in any of the many available after-market link-to-link sets.

Take special care to ensure the running gear is properly aligned to accept the tracks. As the glue sets, run a straight-edge flat against the wheels to check for small inaccuracies that may loom large after the model is finished. Such care is all the more critical with the complicated, interleaved road wheels of the Panther series of tanks *(above)*.

The tracks in place, with spare links for stowage on the superstructure *(right)*. One liability of styrene link-to-link tracks is that they may contract and warp during assembly, while the glue is curing. This effect can pull the drive sprockets and idlers away from the hull and noticeably bend them out of alignment. As you assemble them, check for shrinking link runs. If necessary, wedge basswood chips between the newly-assembled track lengths, drive sprockets or idlers, and the hull sides to prevent distortion as the glue dries.

Assembly Notes, Continued: The Heart of the Beast

I elected to build my Zerstörer with the suggestion of an interior. Dragon's Jagdtiger 12.8 cm gun breech was used as the central assembly for the fictitious fighting compartment of the Zerstörer; as will be seen, a number of other Jagdtiger parts proved useful.

Internal Affairs: The finished cupola interior, ready for painting. The various parts have been placed with reference to the layout of the Panther G cupola, but arranged to conform to the superstructure's shape.
Some of this gear relates to the infrared optical device that will be mounted atop the cupola. Below the tan resin MG 34 ammo bags is the IR maintenance box *(center of picture). Right:* Solder was used for the wire leads running down from the IR gear along the cupola wall.

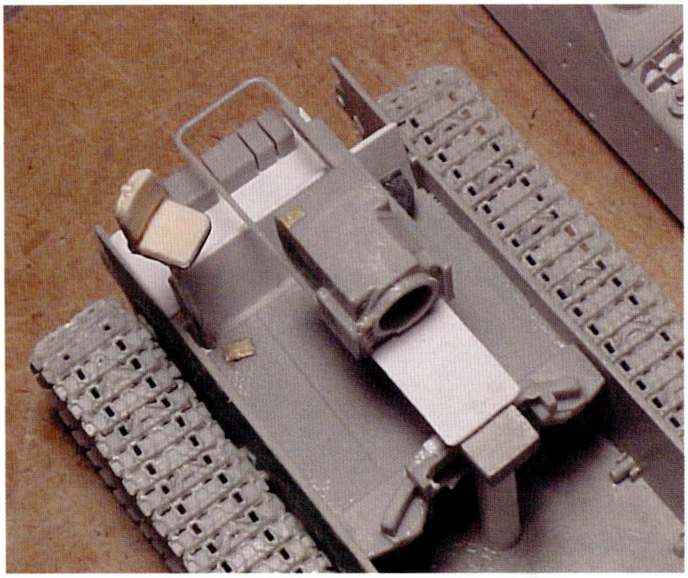

Compartmentalized Thinking: The interior detailing, underway. The features are of course speculative, inspired by those of the Jagdtiger. In fact, a floor section from the Dragon Jagdtiger kit has been cut to size and placed as a foundation for the breech assembly. Again, this was a matter of patiently cutting and testing the fit until the floor was not only level, but sufficiently elevated to line the breech and gun barrel up with the aperture in the Hobbymodellbau superstructure.
The tan resin commander's seat is an after-market accessory, detailed with a lead foil cushion support and suspended from the hull floor with a section of scale metal tubing.

The hull with completed partial interior, painted and ready to accept the Hobbymodellbau resin superstructure.
The acrylic and oil painting techniques employed here are covered in the individual project essays to follow.

Assembly Notes, Continued: The Demands of New and Exotic Research

Afterburners: Having connected the superstructure to the hull as soon as the interior was complete, my attention then turned to the smaller details of the Zerstörer's exterior. I used the Dragon Panther F's muffler mounts, measuring and fitting them to the Hobbymodellbau conversion's rear plate.

Extrapolate, Extrapolate: The model shown on the Hobbymodellbau kit box displays no travel lock for the enormous 12.8 cm gun. Since the Jagdtiger was equipped with one, I thought it safe to assume that the Zerstörer would have carried its own travel lock. After all, a gun tube so long and heavy would likely have to be secured in transit, type of chassis notwithstanding. And the Zerstörer's rear-mounted configuration would have probably made a travel lock all the more likely.
Once more, the parts for the lock were taken from the Dragon Jagdtiger. To connect the A-frame lock assembly to the Panther glacis plate, styrene bits and bolts were used to fashion the hinges, and these were in turn anchored in place with A+B epoxy putty weld points.

I considered using either the Dragon mufflers *(grey)* or resin after-market spares. The resin ones seemed too futuristic and sporty, particularly since they would be highly visible on their mounting points, so I opted to use the Dragon mufflers. This was one occasion when an eye for aesthetics won out over the measurements of a ruler.

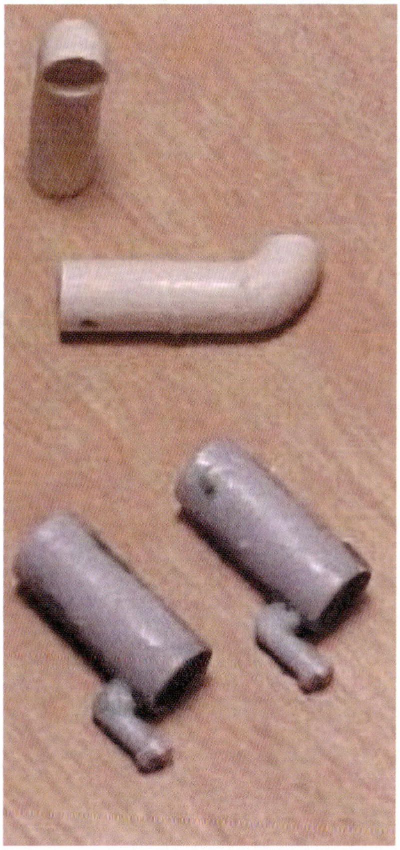

The gun travel lock and engine deck detailing, complete. Note the turned aluminum gun barrel of the conversion kit.

Assembly Notes, Continued: Topping Off the Tank

Two parts from the Dragon Panther F stand in for the **Tamiya** parts called for by the conversion kit. The grey disk is the cover of the roof ventilator, and the other part is the armored periscope cover.

Hooked Up: Small photo-etch tie-down rings from **Scale Model Accessories** were affixed along the edge of the superstructure roof. As on so many actual panzers, these would have made convenient attachment points for crew items, such as helmets, water bottles, etc. Although not visible here, tie-down rings were also placed around the outer lip of the cupola. Note that **Squadron** Green Putty has been used to simulate the welds which secure these rings to the armor plating beneath them.

The styrene radio antenna base is a leftover from a Dragon kit.

Discussion: Cyanoacrylate ("super") glue is the adhesive of choice for bonding styrene, resin, and pieces of photo-etch metal. In most cases, I use the slow-drying, gap-filling formula because it allows enough time to properly position parts before it sets.

The left side vision port plug. The body of the plug was made from styrene tubing, the chain connection point from lead foil and wire, the crown from A+B epoxy putty, and the chain is the very fine kind used by ship modelers.

Reference Materials for Small Details: Achtung Panzer

As has already been noted, trips to ordnance museums afford unique opportunities to research AFVs, and are particularly useful for gaining the "soldier's eye view" perspective, from which even the tiniest of vehicle details can be seen and appreciated.

An equally valuable source, especially if you are not convenient to a museum, is the Japanese *Achtung Panzer* book series from Dai Nippon Kaiga. Lavishly and meticulously illustrated, each title in this series describes one or more panzers in every minute detail. Although *Achtung Panzer* typically includes photographs from ordnance museums, its true value resides in its copious illustrations. These drawings are often given in exact 1/35 scale and cover all the known variants of their subjects. Each panzer's features, including equipment stowage and field modifications, are presented as they evolved during the life of the vehicle, accompanied by production dates and notes about the manufacturers' methods. Such source material makes it simple to model not only highly accurate AFVs, but entirely unique ones, as well.

There is, however, a catch: this series is not cheap. But because each title covers its subjects so comprehensively and authoritatively, *Achtung Panzer* is *de rigeur* to the model panzer enthusiast.

For the Zerstörer, I consulted *Achtung Panzer #4: Panther, Jagdpanther & Brummbaer*. This title furnished essential information for fabricating parts like the pistol port plug *(above)*.

Just as valuable to the panzer modeler is his cache of spare parts. Over the years, I have accumulated lots of vehicle details. Some, like this jack from **Gunze Sangyo's** Jagdpanther, are simply exquisite. Working from *Achtung Panzer* drawings, I added a lead foil base plate and styrene butterfly nut to an already formidable accessory to produce a jack for the Zerstörer's equipment suite.

Left: A wash with dark brown hobby acrylic shows off the fine weld beads of the cupola and its "pulpit," as well as the interlock joints of the rolled steel armor plate. It's hard to find such crisp, well-rendered detail in most styrene kits.

A Note About Photo-Etch Accessories

Photo-etch detailing accessories emerged during the AFV after-market explosion of the 1980s. Because photo-etch involves fabricating details from wafer-thin frets of brass or nickel parts, its foremost advantage is that it permits the AFV modeler to construct fenders, machine gun shields, tie-down clasps, etc. in scale thicknesses that are more accurate than can be found with styrene parts. As will be seen, it has also made possible new techniques for depicting battle damage. It's ironic that this virtually two-dimensional product has, in a figurative sense, added yet another dimension to modeling.

Photo-etch accessory sets fairly bristle with parts—sometimes hundreds—and some of these can be minuscule. Do not feel obligated to use every one. Sometimes, elaborate photo-etch subassemblies can take hours to construct, without substantially improving upon the kit parts they were designed to replace.

Photo-etch is but one of many means to an end. Ultimately, it's for you alone to decide whether your investment of time and effort will make a particular super-detailing project worthwhile. Bear in mind that painstaking photo-etch work does not by itself make for a particularly realistic model. The most intricate handiwork can easily be hidden under a single, cursory coat of paint.

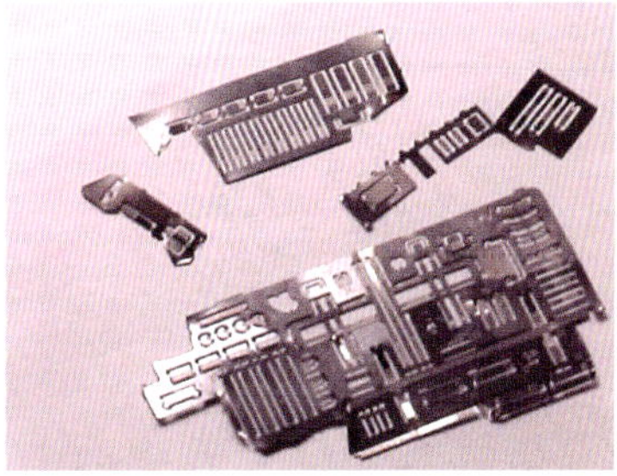

Because the Zerstörer would have been based upon a later Pz.Kpfw. V Panther series chassis, useful photo-etch parts were found in **Eduard's** 1/35 Panther G set.

Frequently, sets designed for a particular styrene kit will work just as well with similar kits from other manufacturers.

Short lengths of spare track will be hung along the Zerstörer's superstructure on superbly delicate photo-etch hooks. Some years ago, before the advent of photo-etch, I fashioned these very details for a Panther G from scratch, expending a lot of time and energy in the process.

Shrapnel Warning: One frustrating characteristic of photo-etch parts is their tendency to fly off of the worktable when being cut or trimmed. *Exercise care when removing photo-etch parts from their frets. Wear glasses to protect your eyes from flying flecks of metal during the cutting.* Cupping your free hand over the immediate work area *(above)* helps to prevent "tweezer launch," as photo-etch stalwarts have come to call it. Secure loose parts to the table with small loops of masking tape so they won't disappear during assembly. Tiny bits of brass and nickel have a reflective quality that makes them hard to spot on a hard floor, and nearly impossible to retrieve from a carpet.

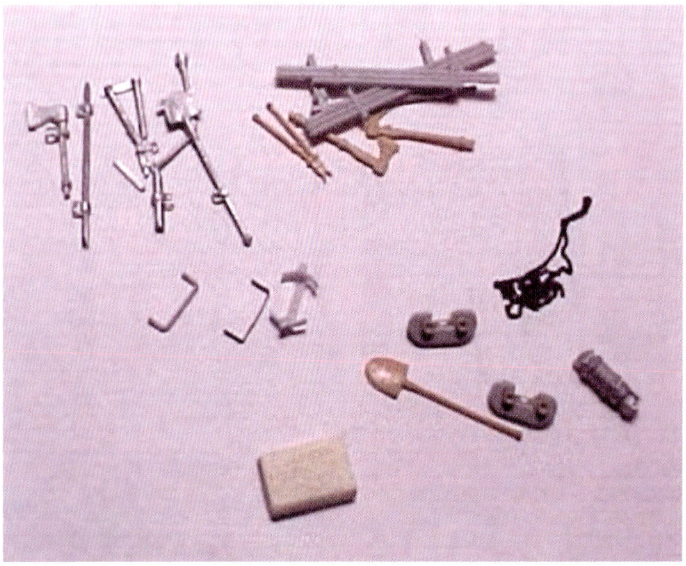

Stock Options: On-vehicle equipment, waiting to be augmented with photo-etch and scratch-built hasps and clamps for mounting on the vehicle.

To the standard panzer gear, such as shovels, axes, a wood jack block, and a fire extinguisher, I have added items from the Panther series that would have been just as useful to the crew of the Zerstörer: towing clevises and a scratch-built track-changing cable bracket.

For the Zerstörer I chose tow cables from **Hudson & Allen Studios**, an innovative maker of AFV kit accessories. These cables come with an already rusty finish, and are flexible enough to fit around the contours of any AFV model.

Assembly Notes, Continued: The Walk-Around

Suite Emotion: Working from photos of the Pz.Kpfw. V Jagdpanther at Aberdeen Proving Ground, I fashioned the port hull side tool bracket from lengths of **Evergreen** styrene strip. The weld points that secured the real thing to the superstructure have again been simulated with Squadron Green Putty.
Note the vision pistol port plug (discussed at p. 18) hanging by its chain from the open port at upper right.

The port side vehicle tools, in place. The clamps and fasteners of the tools were modeled with a combination of styrene, spare photo-etch, and shaped lead foil parts; copper wires of two different gauges comprise each towing clevis' pins and its retaining lead. A circular late-production tow cable retainer *(white disk on glacis corner)* was punched from thin styrene.

Candle in the Wind *(Right)*: The "Bosch" headlight mount was made from a sheet styrene shelf and a mounting socket from another kit. As with the port and starboard tool arrays, a close-up look at the Aberdeen Jagdpanther's light mount provided valuable information.

Left: The starboard tool bracket. The hull machine gun barrel in its domed mount is from **Collectors Brass**, a company that specializes in this kind of accessory.
Lower Left: The starboard tools, underway. Note that on this side the spare parts used are largely white metal and resin. Again, I have employed lead foil in place of photo-etch to simplify some tasks. The large tan piece of resin is the wood block used for supporting the vehicle's jack.

Discussion: As the last few photos illustrate, super-detailing needn't be limited to working with photo-etch. Although a good photo-etch accessory set by itself can dramatically improve an AFV kit, I like to mix in other materials whenever doing so will hasten assembly without compromising detail.

Left: Additional multi-media tools and fixtures. The item at far right is the track changing cable bracket of the Panther series. The tiny brass chain dangling from it came from an **Aber** photo-etch accessory set. I bent it to hang properly and twisted it slightly to give it a three-dimensional look.

The port and starboard side superstructure details, complete. Note how the tow cables have been fastened along the sloping sides of the Zerstörer.

Take Me to Your Leader: Since this model portrays a hypothetical command vehicle, it would properly have been designated *Zerstörer Befehlswagen*. Wartime photos show the large, collapsible antenna mast in use on at least one late-model Panther G, making it a probable feature of the command Zerstörer.

Here, the antenna mast has been placed temporarily in its mount on the left rear corner of the superstructure. For ease of handling, the mast assembly was left unattached until painting was finished.

Discussion: Several different materials went into the construction of the antenna mount: a modified styrene kit part, styrene tubing, aluminum sheet, two plies of a fine lead solder strand, and **Grandt Line** and **Modelkasten** wing nuts. The radio mast itself was made from a **Plastruct** styrene tube, detailed at five points with lead foil to represent the field assembly joints. When you begin with reasonably detailed source materials and are willing to indulge in some educated extrapolation, subassemblies like this antenna mast make exotic panzer projects all the more satisfying.

Putting Out Feelers: I elected to model a command vehicle, so extra antennae were needed for this Zerstörer. The "crow's foot" array *(upper right)* was typical of German command tanks; this one is a photo-etch accessory from **Accurate Armor**.

The construction of the thick, telescoping radio mast *(lower right)* is described next.

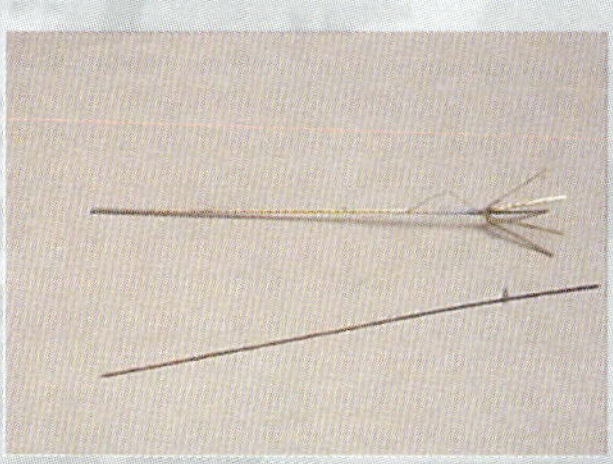

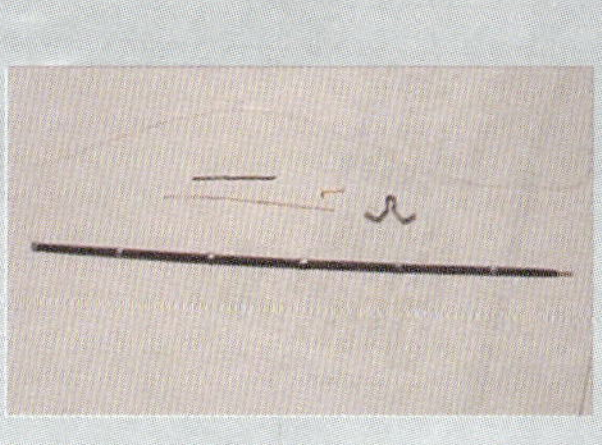

Finishing Notes: Painting, Marking, and Weathering

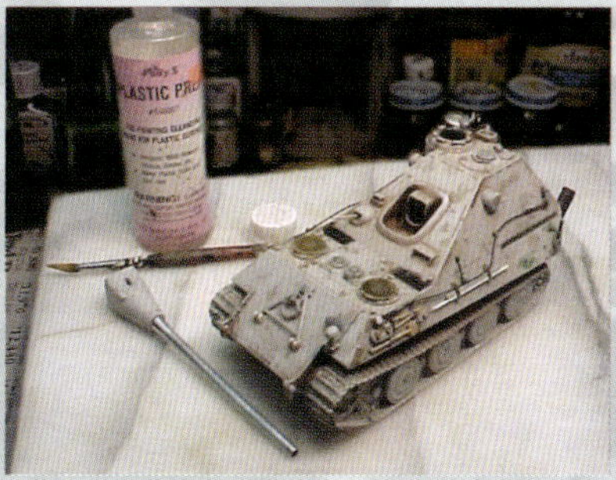

The completed vehicle was liberally brushed with **Polly S.** Plastic Prep to ensure clean surfaces for painting. Although there will always be some parts better left off the vehicle during painting, try to assemble as much of the model as is practicable beforehand.

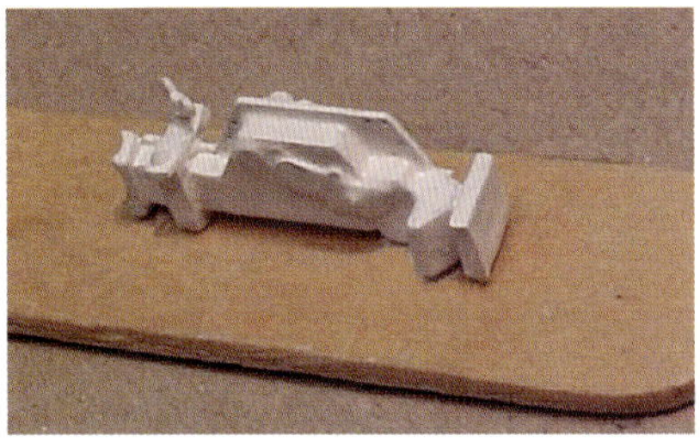

I sealed the various assemblies for painting with a light coat of lacquer primer *(upper right)*. **Floquil's** Base White Primer spray is perfect for this, though in some cases their Base Black is more useful, as with vehicles colored Panzer Grey.
Note that the gun barrel is masked with tape for separate handling, and that a piece of rolled paper was inserted into the open cupola to protect the completed interior from primer over-spray.
Middle and lower right: The infrared array and the jack have likewise been primed with light sprays, followed by thin coats of Floquil brush-on primer. Careful brush painting helped to minimize the risk of damaging the delicate IR gear and ensured that both pieces were thoroughly coated.

Compared with today's inexpensive and quiet hobby compressors, my old 1/2 h.p. **Sears** unit is noisy and over-powered, but still quite reliable. A pressure regulator attachment gives the airbrush a useful working range, between 10 and 30 psi.

Plotting and Scheming: Throughout World War Two, the German armed forces—the *Waffen-SS*, in particular—experimented ceaselessly with techniques of camouflage. I took this phenomenon as a point of departure for a hypothetical vehicle scheme based upon the proven late-war *Waffen-SS* "summer oakleaf" uniform pattern (*see p. 47*). The concept at work here is that the Zerstörer's battalion workshop has used the three standard panzer camouflage colors authorized in early 1943, but has mixed them and applied them to mimic the subtleties found in the "summer oakleaf" uniform pattern.
Before beginning the camouflage itself, I sprayed the recesses, undersurfaces, and areas of shadow on the Zerstörer with a warm, deep brown tone mixed from Tamiya acrylic colors: three parts XF-10 Dark Brown to two parts XF-1 Black.
The camouflaging process is described next.

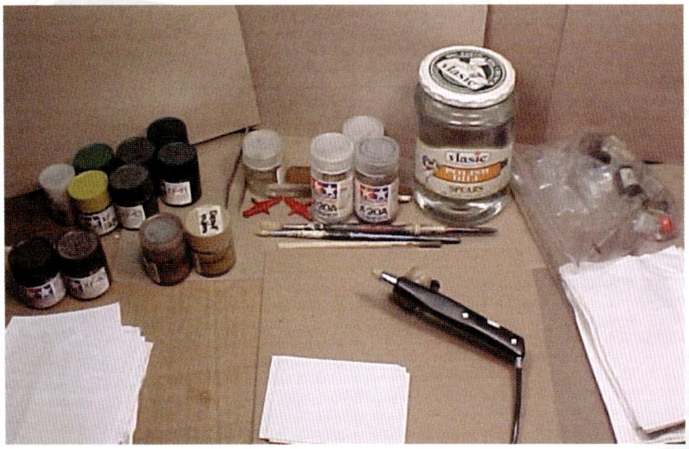

Wind Tunnel: For airbrushing, a cardboard screen has been set up to isolate the worktable and contain the spray fumes. I use a **Modelmaster** double-action airbrush, as well as the accessories pictured: Tamiya acrylic colors and thinner; scraps of white printing paper for checking colors and for practicing painting techniques; a large jar of water for acrylic clean-up; brushes and stirrers for mixing paint; tools for maintaining the airbrush; and a sandwich bag for holding additional airbrushing supplies.

Step One: The workshop painters have chosen to deepen the basic dark yellow color by adding an equal portion of red brown. The base color of the model, then, is a 1:1 mix of Tamiya XF-59 Desert Yellow and XF-64 Red Brown.

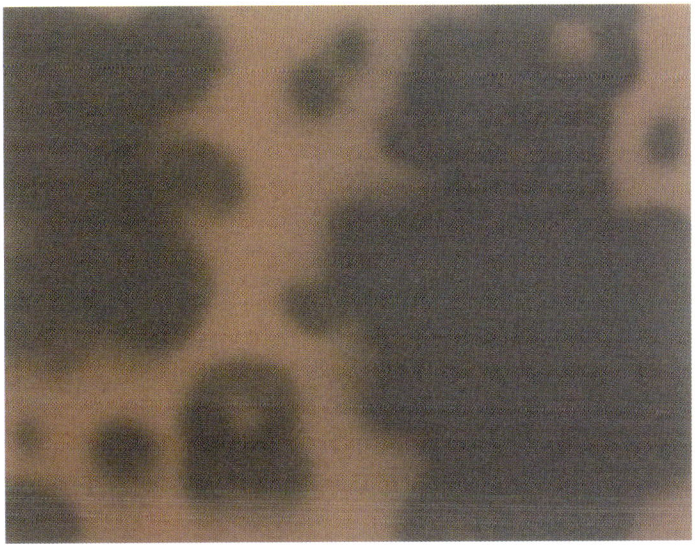

Step Two: The first over-sprayed color is dark olive green, using Tamiya XF-13 J.A. Green. Here, the painters have started their experiment by applying opaque shapes, using a borrowed camouflage smock or tent as a guide.

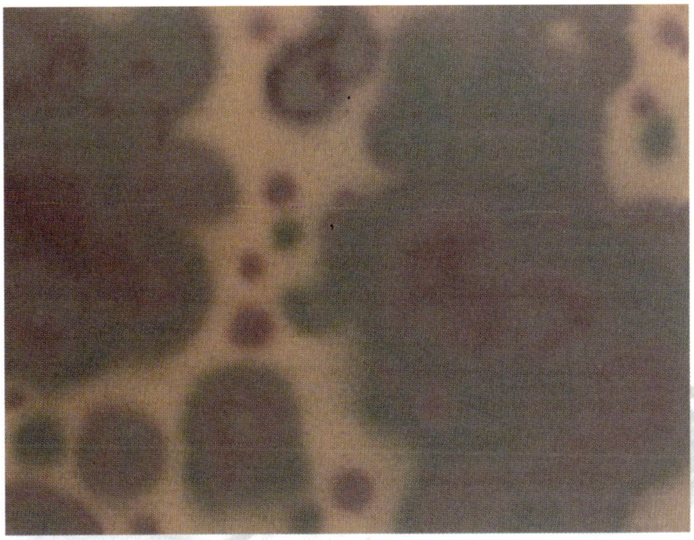

Step Three: The second over-spray, Tamiya XF-10 Flat Brown, represents a deep, concentrated application of armor red brown. It overlaps the dark olive green in roughly equal measure, and small spots have been sprayed around the dark green, on the base sand brown.

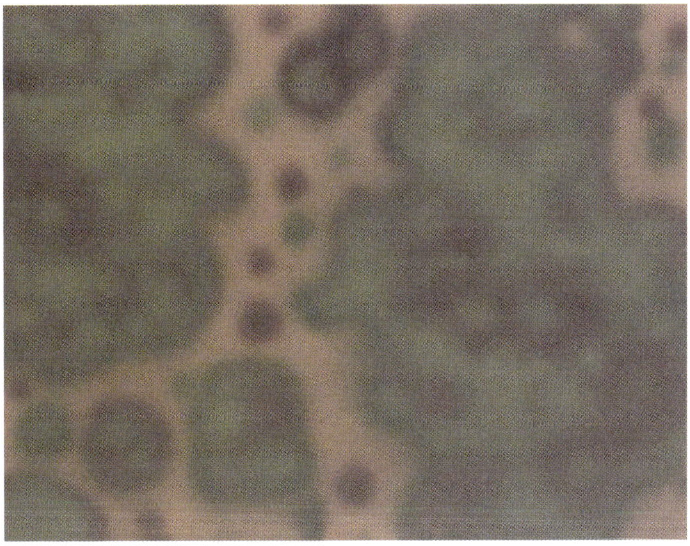

Step Four: After again carefully examining their source fabric, the workshop painters have mixed a third camouflage color from dark yellow (Tamiya XF-60) and dark olive green, giving a medium olive green tone. This they've sprayed more sparingly, into and around the colors already laid in.

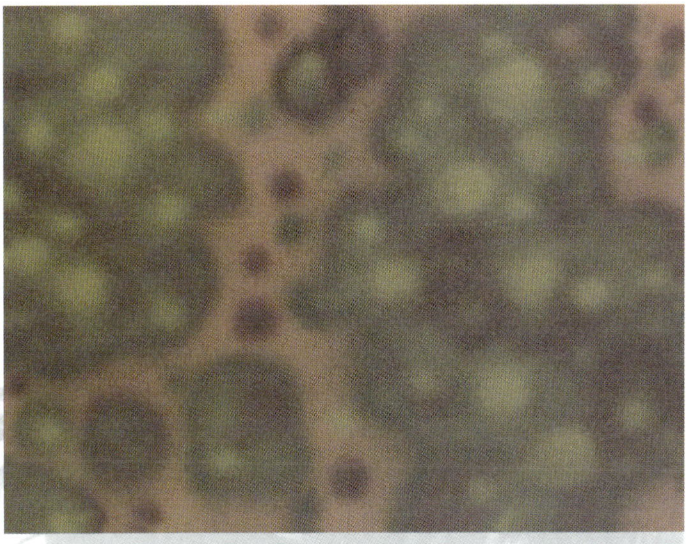

Step Five: The final camouflage color is a vibrant pea green, mixed again from dark yellow and dark olive green, but this time in a 4:1 ratio.
With this last application, the workshop painters pack up their equipment and speculate about how well their innovative new scheme will help to conceal the Zerstörer.

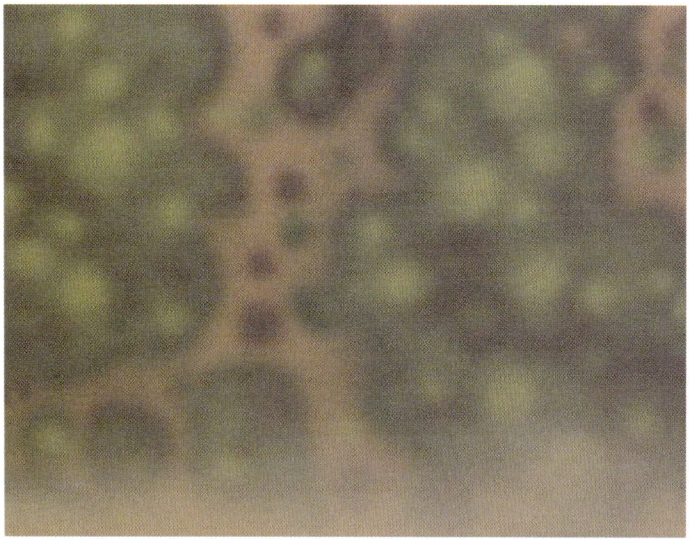

. . .Dust to Dust: During the weathering process, the Modelmaster airbrush was used to impart a dust effect to the lower areas of the Zerstörer. The result is illustrated by the color swatch shown above.
First, Tamiya XF-52 Flat Earth was lightly sprayed in a translucent cloud that tapers off as it rises up the vehicle's sides. Next, the same color lightened with XF-57 Buff was applied, this time more sparingly to the upper reaches but more heavily along the lower edge, creating a realistic variation in the dust effect.

Eye Surgery: The commander's infrared suite was one of those fragile sub-assemblies that I treated as a model in its own right. To avoid damaging it, I painted it separately and attached it only at the last moment.

The completed "oak leaf" camouflage scheme.

Discussion: Because the airbrush does its job so fast and so well, uniform coverage is easy to achieve. However, uniformity is usually not desirable when your object is to simulate the irregularities of hand-sprayed camouflage and natural weathering effects.
Above: The "dusting" technique, as applied to the right rear sponson edge of the finished Zerstörer. Notice how the extent of the dust effect has been varied along the edge, adding complexity to the otherwise simple, linear qualities of the superstructure.
While this kind of subtlety is possible with a single-action airbrush, it is much easier to do with a double-action one like the Modelmaster.

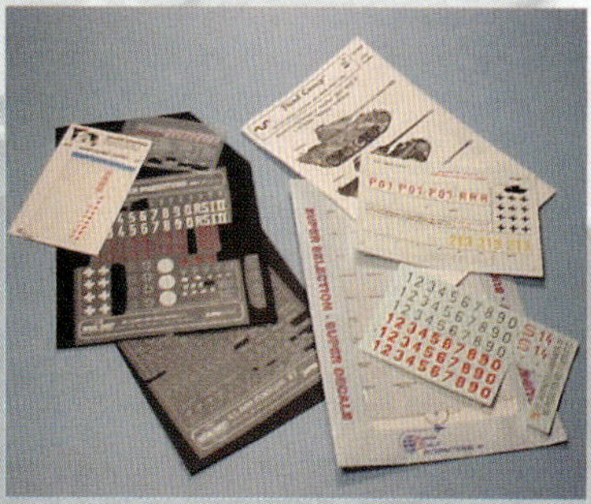

Decalcomania: One of the fringe benefits of working with a more or less mythical AFV design is the relative freedom to choose how to mark it. For the Zerstörer, I selected markings from among various brands of conventional water-emulsion decals and dry transfers *(left)*, as well as photo-etched stencils from **Cromwell** or **Stencil-It** *(right)*.

Finishing Notes, Continued: Completing the Zerstörer
(Note: the techniques used for painting and weathering are discussed in detail in the project essays to follow.)

The finished hull front. The friction of recent road travel has polished the cleats of the otherwise rusty track links to a bright luster. This effect was simulated with silver paint.

Making Your Mark: The Zerstörer's front corner insignia consist of a **Verlinden Productions** dry transfer *balkankreuz* (German cross), a **Super Scale Decals** tactical sign, and a hand-painted pink *Panzerkorps* symbol (a jagged "S").
Discussion: There are four different media currently available for marking AFVs:
Traditional water-emulsion decals have steadily evolved in terms of both image quality and ease of use. However, to mask the decal film's inherent sheen and to give a uniform, "painted-on" look, the whole vehicle must be varnished with premium-quality flat clear.
Dry transfers have the advantage of looking like scale paint and usually require no covering varnish, but they are difficult to position, particularly on irregular surfaces.
Photo-etch stencils for airbrushing or hand-painting markings also confer the look of scale paint. They are easy to position on broad, flat surfaces, but are nearly impossible to position anywhere else.
Enamel or acrylic hobby paints are at once the most flexible yet time-consuming alternative. They can be hand-brushed onto light pencil lines, into stencils fashioned from masking tape, and even over existing decals, but in any event require a steady, precise hand.

This *Abteilung* command vehicle bears a typical double-digit "01" designation. The number appears in black, under the gun trunnion caps on both sides. These dry transfers were burnished onto the superstructure, taking care not to damage the clasps, tow cables, or foliage rings.

The completed port and starboard on-vehicle gear.

Rust occurs in different ways on operational AFVs. Here, the unused spare track links have completely rusted over, and now lack the reflective qualities of bare metal. But the muffler cylinders, which are subject to a continuous routine of heating up and cooling down, have been painted to appear to be in the process of rusting. This was done by mixing warm metallic oil and enamel tones into the rust-colored paint.

The Zerstörer's wheels are the later all-metal model from the Panther series, which lack rubber tires. Continuous contact with the tracks and road obstacles has caused the paint to chip and flake away. However, repeated running has prevented rust from forming on the exposed metal of the contact points. To learn how these wheels would have looked in use, I studied wartime photos of similar wheels on late model Tiger and Tiger II tanks.

Sometimes Less is More: I chose to leave off the track-changing cable to show more of the fixture around which it would have been wrapped *(center, with dangling chain)*. Note how the stretch of tow cable has a patina of rust, but the more frequently used rack tools *(left)* are almost a bare metal color.

. . .And Sometimes More is More: As the Zerstörer is not engaged in combat, its MG 34 machine gun probably would not have been left in its mount, at least not without a protective canvas cover. Because it was worth showing, I took some artistic license.

Bitter Irony: This meticulously-painted heavy tank destroyer has recently had its gun barrel replaced; it has yet to be painted and is just now beginning to rust. Such anomalies were not unusual at the end of World War Two, and probably would have gone on into 1946 had the Third Reich made a last desperate stand.

Finishing Notes: The Human Touch

Behold the Man: This bespectacled tanker is not only the vehicle commander, but a *standartenführer* of the *Waffen-SS*. Such a rank often held a regimental command within a panzer division. But this officer has been entrusted with the command of an elite, independent Zerstörer *Abteilung*, temporarily attached to an *SS Panzerkorps*.
A remarkable number of *Waffen-SS* soldiers survived close to six years of fierce and uninterrupted fighting, only to end the war as high-ranking field commanders in charge of small formations—some of which, though lacking in equipment, were still highly motivated and battle-worthy.

The commander's infrared device is now permanently attached to the cupola.
The barely visible details of the interior of the cupola drum and fighting compartment act as a draw to the viewer; hopefully, their visual elusiveness will inspire fascination.

The *standartenführer* assesses the situation with a map board and motorcycle dispatch from *SS Panzerkorps* headquarters.

A Man, a Heavy Tank Destroyer, and a Plan: Zerstörer!

With the Zerstörer now complete, the first of two crewmen intended for display on the vehicle has taken his place on the roof. The construction and painting of the second is detailed in the next project essay, *A Soldier's Story*.

-EFM

A Soldier's Story

Constructing, Modifying, and Painting a Waffen-SS Tank Crewman

IN CHAPTER ONE, WE DISCUSSED MODELING AN EXOTIC panzer. We outlined some useful techniques for assembling, modifying, and super-detailing a project that featured a wide (and perhaps intimidating) array of modeling materials. Starting with a styrene plastic AFV and an epoxy resin conversion kit, we added photo-etch accessories, solder, brass rod, copper wiring, epoxy putty enhancements, and so on to make the Zerstörer. And, as with the exotic panzers to follow, we employed some study and speculation to put into three dimensions what began only as a blueprint.

Now, let's turn to "the human element": the 1/35 scale figure, and its role in the composition of an AFV diorama or vignette.

The addition of miniature human forms to an AFV model display effectively transforms it from a static replica of a combat vehicle into a "happening." At their most basic, miniature figures provide a valuable scale reference that informs the viewer of the real-life size of a particular vehicle. But when used more ambitiously, figures can become the most eloquent components of your projects. Rarely can an inanimate object in a diorama describe an event, or convey a mood, or even express profound truth, as effectively as miniature human forms, provided they are well planned and executed. Ever since early peoples started to scrape imitations of the things they saw around them onto the walls of caves, humans have returned again and again to the subject that fascinates them most: themselves. This fascination is no less a part of the miniature art than it is of painting, sculpture, or for that matter, cinema.

As well as contributing vitality, storytelling power, and historical context to your AFV projects, the process of planning figures into your scenes is a useful creative exercise. While an AFV model standing alone can impress, rarely does it stimulate the viewer's imagination. On the other hand, the decision to incorporate figures into your AFV scenes opens up unlimited modeling possibilities. In a nutshell, it takes people to make the machines of war move. When they are missing, their absence is conspicuous; when they are present, *anything can happen*.

Although the focus of this essay is on modifying and enhancing a commercially available 1/35 scale figure, it should be noted that there is nowadays an excellent selection of stock figures available for use in dioramas and vignettes. Whether molded in styrene, resin, or white metal, the figures of the present generation are a far cry from those of only twenty-five years ago; measured by today's standards, those were more akin to toy soldiers than realistic miniature sculptures. Styrene figure sets especially have come into their own in terms of both molding quality and imaginative posing, and their sharp prices make them all the more appealing.

So take heart—if your preference is more for modeling the machines of war than their human masters, you will be awestruck by the broad variety of imaginative stock figures waiting to be painted, and if used thoughtfully they will complement any panzer.

But there is still a special satisfaction to be found in modifying available figures to suit your own ideas. Even minor alterations can result in a more appropriate uniform, engaging gesture, or interesting personality. Hence, the photo essay that follows, chronicling the process of transforming a commercial figure into a unique panzer crewman for the Zerstörer: an *obersturmfuehrer* of the 1st SS Panzer Division.

The "Before" Photo: *This project began with a figure by* ***Dragon*** *from their Tiger Aces set. The box illustration depicts a late-war tanker in typical SS "pea pattern" camouflage uniform, and closely resembles the actual styrene plastic figure. Dragon offers an incredibly broad range of fine figures.*

One for the Books: Publications, videotaped documentaries, and even written accounts without photos are at least as valuable for modeling soldiers as they are for vehicles. For checking the accuracy of a figure's uniform and gear details, some of the best sources are color pictorials produced by memorabilia collectors and re-enactment groups. For direct inspiration, film footage of actual soldiers is ideal. A few minutes of viewing a good documentary helps to remind you of how people actually look and behave. Although the quality of commercial figures is steadily improving, too many manufacturers still limit their figures' poses and gestures to soldiers simply aiming rifles, standing stiffly at attention while conferring over maps, or shouting and pointing towards the horizon for no compelling reason. Such figures do not really animate a scene; they merely populate it. Compare real-life footage of a *panzergrenadier* drinking from his canteen to a typical 1/35 scale figure doing the same thing and you will likely agree.

Let There be Light: To quicken the curing process of epoxy putty to as short as twenty or thirty minutes, a cardboard "light box" lined with aluminum foil and equipped with a 60-watt bulb is very handy. As the inside of the box can reach 150 degrees Fahrenheit, extreme care must be exercised when working with assemblies that combine epoxy putty and other materials. Styrene plastic and delicate resin parts warp and melt with prolonged exposure to heat. Many of your figure projects may begin with plastic parts, so you will want to invest in a kitchen timer *(right)* to eliminate the risk of leaving things in the box for too long.

Schiffer's *Sculpting Miniature Military Figures* by Kim Jones gives further details about using light boxes. It is also an excellent source for learning how to create scale figures with epoxy putty.

Tools essential to figure modification include: epoxy putty; fine steel wool; lacquer thinner or water as a wetting agent; and of all things, old scrapers and picks acquired from a generous dentist. These last items may be too worn for use on human teeth, but they make excellent tools for sculpting epoxy putty.

Dragon's "Tiger Ace" is typical of the newest and best of the styrene plastic figures. The pose is natural, with the hands placed casually on the hips rather than cupped awkwardly out into space, as is so often seen with older figures. Note the pronounced wrinkling of the jacket and trousers. Although his boots are slightly small, this soldier has plenty of promise.

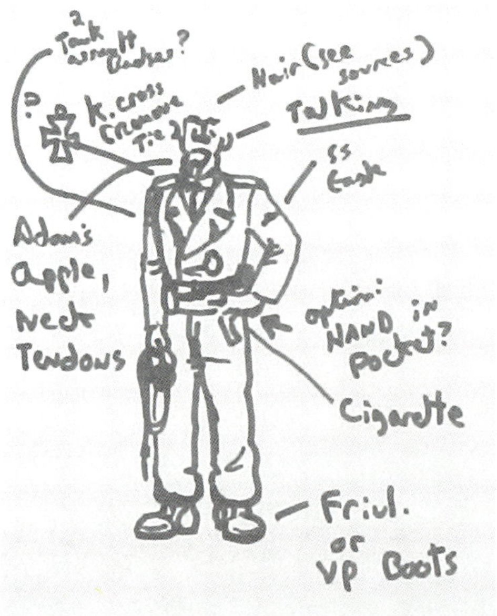

At the outset, it is helpful (but not necessary) to produce a rough sketch of the figure as you want it to appear in its final form. The quality of this sketch is not critical, so long as it lets you settle upon the pose or gesture. It's also convenient for consolidating notes about the details you intend to incorporate. My notes in the drawing include plans to change the figure's boots and to give it a bare head with sculpted hair.

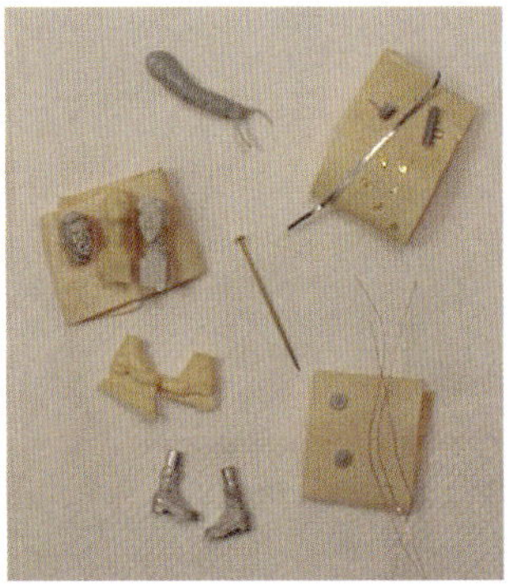

Potentially useful accessories are laid out for consideration. Among these are replacement heads from **Friulmodellismo**, **Hornet**, and **Wolf**; **Verlinden** boots; a Dragon arm from the same set; lead foil strips; and copper wire. The straight pin is for attachment to the base.

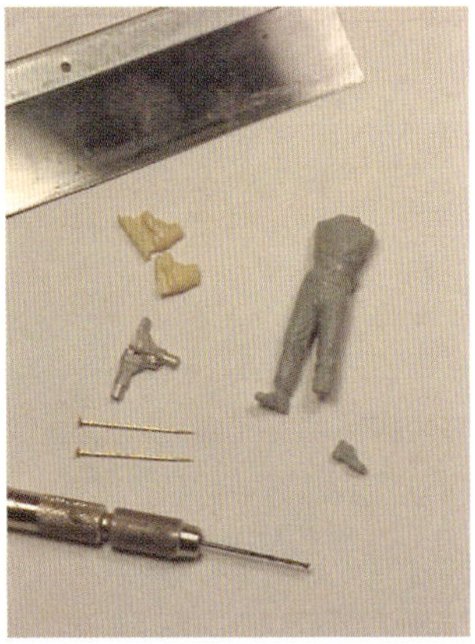

The styrene figure's boots were sawed off with a fine-tooth razor saw. At this point, I was still deciding which pair of replacement feet to use. I went with the metal Friul. boots because of their crisp laces and soles, as well as their appropriately bulky look. While the molded plastic boots were under-scale, these sized up very well.

Black Ties and Tails: The uniforms worn by German tankers were designed to be practical and comfortable, but countless photos like the above verify that crewmen were frequently issued ill-fitting jackets or trousers, and that uninterrupted wear under tough field conditions could take its toll on even the most resilient of fabrics. Indeed, wartime photographs make clear that a poor uniform fit was more the rule than the exception, particularly as the war progressed and the tide began to turn for Germany.

Note the bagginess of the trouser seats and cuffs, and the wrinkles running through the back of the nearest tanker's jacket *(far right)*.

Although these men appear to be dressed in the typical faded black panzer outfit, the same effects can be seen in photos of soldiers wearing camouflage uniforms, as well.

The larger parts of the figure have been assembled and mounted on a 2" by 2" block. These inexpensive wood cubes make ideal handholds for painting small-scale figures, and can be purchased at most craft supply shops. The white square is a piece of printer paper, white-glued to the block.

A Note About Attaching Figures to Painting Bases

I use lengths of headless straight pins to connect 1/35 scale figures to their painting blocks. For a plastic or resin figure, one length of pin in the heel of the more firmly grounded foot should suffice; for a heavier lead alloy figure, a pin in each foot may be needed. Although a pin vise can be used to drill the mounting hole in the base, a power **Dremel** tool on a low speed setting is faster, safe for your figure, and much easier on your wrists.

Drill a hole in the base through the paper, then glue the pin into the figure's foot with two-part epoxy glue. Insert this pin into the hole in the base with cyanoacrylate ("super") glue. Put the glue between the sole of the foot and the paper. When finished, the figure will easily peel away from the base, any residual paper can be trimmed away from the sole, and the pin in the heel can then be used to anchor the figure to the final display base.

The two major modifications to the figure are seen here. First, the right arm has been replaced with another from the same Dragon figure set. This arm hangs at the side and holds the frame of a radio headset.
Second, a resin head from Wolf has been substituted for the styrene head. This new "shouting" head has been angled upward to suit the position the crewman will be taking atop his vehicle.

I wanted to equip the *obersturmführer* with not only his headset, but the throat microphone and wires that go along with it. Fine copper speaker wire strands were used to form the cables connecting the headset and the figure's throat-phone assembly (*see finished figure, p. 38*). Another strand was wrapped into a loose, dangling loop behind the headset frame to simulate the bunched-up stretch of cable that connects to the vehicle radio set.
Note that epoxy putty has been used to fill out the trouser cuffs, and to smooth the connection between the boots and trousers.

While I admired the shouting expression of the Wolf head, its skull seemed too small, with the ears set too far forward. **A+B** Epoxy putty was used to re-sculpt both features. The hair was added separately *(below)*.

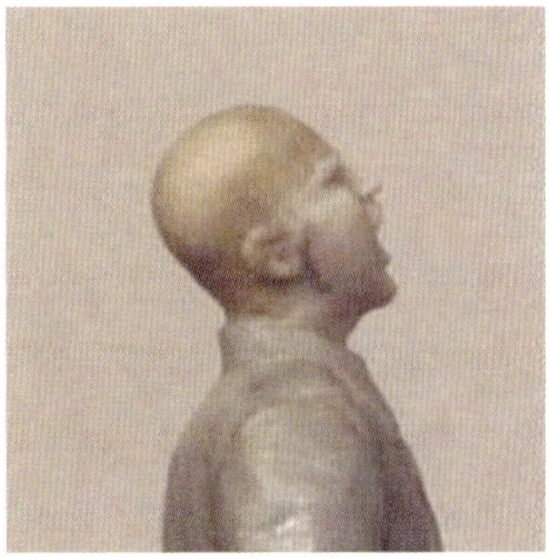

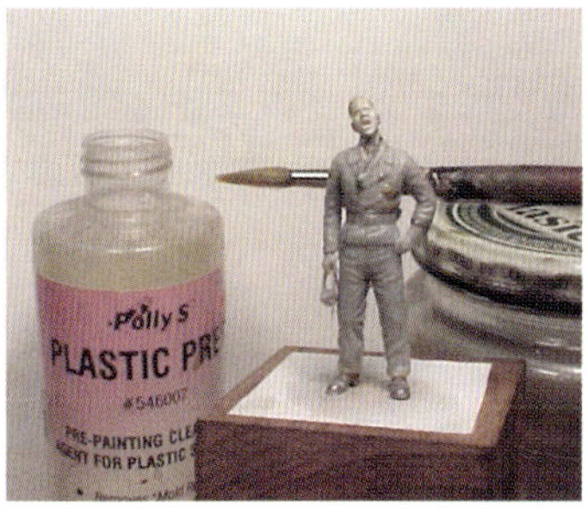

I applied **Polly S.** Plastic Prep solution to the miniature to ensure a clean surface for priming *(left)*. Before dusting the figure with several light coats of **Floquil** White Primer, I brush-painted the white metal boots to more thoroughly seal them for the acrylic and oil colors to follow *(right)*.

Mug Shots: If the human form injects vitality into a scale model scene, then the form's face imparts personality and makes it truly unique. It's impossible to give too much consideration to your figure's face, but an often-overlooked aspect of personality is a figure's head of hair.
I chose a distinctive hairstyle, seen in the photo of an officer of a *Waffen-SS* panzer division *(left)* as a pattern for the hair of the modified resin Wolf head *(right)*.
Not only does a detail like this reinforce a figure's uniqueness, it also demonstrates attention to historical accuracy.

Single White Male: Although it is not absolutely critical to undercoat mostly plastic or resin figures, there are good reasons to make a practice of it. First, the white primer helps to show up any flaws in a figure's assembly or rough spots on its surface. Second, a white base surface acts as a "canvas," helping the painter to clearly distinguish color tones as they are applied. In any event, care must be taken to avoid priming the figure too heavily and obscuring fine detail.

Finishing the Obersturmführer

To finish the *obersturmführer*, I employed my "multi-media" painting method, the same as was used on all of the figures seen in this book. This technique takes advantage of the strengths of both water-based acrylic enamels and artists' oil paints.
As you will see, some aspects of the technique are generally applicable and are more or less set in place. However, there's always plenty of room for experimentation.

The Face is Familiar . . . : The more subtle painted effects of the *obersturmführer* will later be accomplished with oil paints. However, it is helpful in the long run to incorporate detail in your figure's faces, hands, and other especially delicate areas during the acrylic under-painting process, so a word or two about fine acrylic painting technique is in order.
When mixing and shading acrylic colors, the advantages of artists' oil paints—smooth blending and a slow drying time—are not available to you. But an impressive degree of subtlety can be obtained with acrylics by using a controlled glazing technique.
This approach to simulating shading and top-lighting on figures uses alternating layers of glazes and opaque paint strokes to "weave" fine gradations between shades within given areas of color. Because glazes alone can take on a coarse, stark quality when dry, additional opaque overlays help to soften the finish.
Discussion: The picture above shows the completed under-painting of the face. Over the base flesh color I applied a deep umber-brown acrylic glaze, let it settle into the recesses for about twenty seconds, then "feathered" away the sharper borders of the glaze color by whisking with a soft, dry #4 sable brush. This first glaze quickly and cleanly defined the figure's facial features. On top of this I applied more of the underlying opaque flesh tone to the raised and naturally sunlit areas of the face (chin, cheekbones, bridge of nose, brow) to further soften the glaze and restore the original tone.
A soft grey-brown glaze was used to add "five o'clock shadow," and a pink glaze helped to define the lips.

Acrylic Underpainting

Because most acrylic hobby paints do not cover particularly well, several coats may be needed to attain an overall opaque undercoat finish on your figure. This is more a matter of patience than technique: allow ample drying time between coats and build up a thin, smooth surface.
A hand-held hair dryer may be used to quicken the drying time between coats.
Such care must be taken because acrylic paints tend to cake up on painted surfaces, depositing minute bumps and flecks that can go unnoticed until it's too late to remove them easily.

The major limitation of acrylic hobby paint is its rapid setting time. Once exposed to air, wet paint begins to acquire a surface film almost immediately.
To retard the drying process and buy yourself more mixing and working time, invest in a "wetting agent," such as the Flow Improver produced by **Winsor & Newton** *(right)*.

The first step in under-painting involves neatly and completely massing in the appropriate base colors of the figure. At right, I have applied the basic flesh tone and delineated the belts, badges, and seams. Now would also be the time to mass in solid-colored jackets and trousers, but the intricate camouflage of this figure demands special treatment.

Painting the Waffen-SS "Pea-Pattern" Camouflage: Step-by-Step

The *obersturmführer* is dressed in a version of camouflage uniform that became available to *Waffen-SS* soldiers later in the war. Known as the "pea pattern" because it featured numerous small, round spots of color, this camouflage is shown being worn by a reenactor in this present-day photo.
As can be seen, bright sunlight adds complexity to an already complex garment by introducing varying degrees of shadow.

The first camouflage "peas" are of a slightly pinkish tan color mixed from sand and flesh paints. The dots are applied in irregular clusters, working the brush in short strokes, and all in the same direction. By using slightly-thinned paint, it is possible to suggest a realistic, "dyed-in-the-fabric" quality *(see color swatch below).*

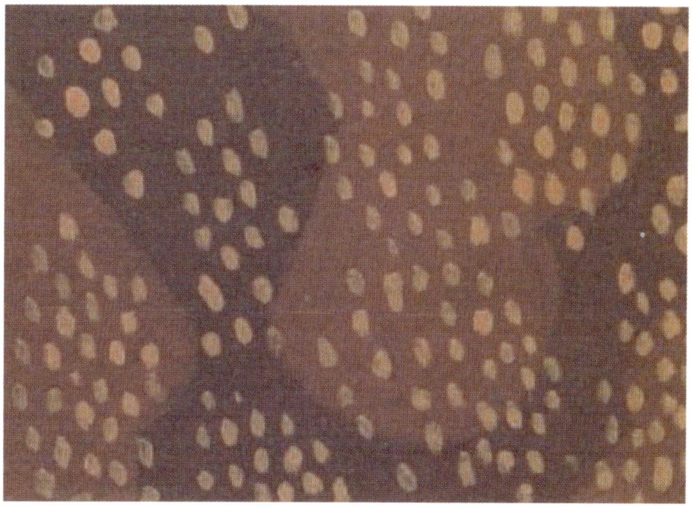

The camouflage of the jacket begins with a cool, medium-dark brown acrylic undercoat.

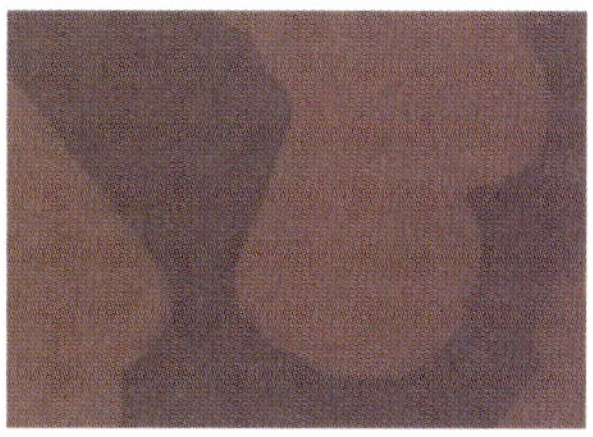

Over this, large patches of a distinctly lighter, warmer brown are painted. The two colors each cover about the same amount of surface area.

Note: added realism is achieved by breaking up the color patches at the garment's seams.

The second layer of "peas" is made up of black-green dots, applied much more sparsely and with even greater variation in the density of the clusters.

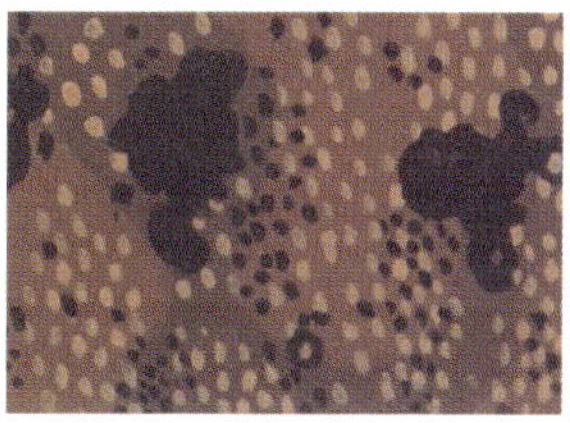

Next, intermediately-sized blotches of the black-green color are applied, taking care not to throw the color proportions out of balance.

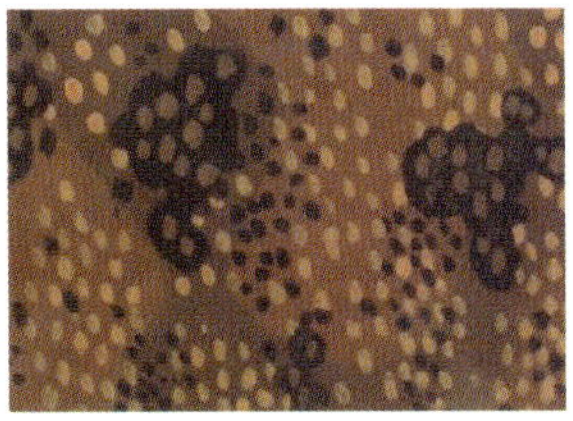

After this, sparse and irregular clusters of the original sand/flesh-tone dots are brought back onto the black-green areas.

Completing the Obersturmführer: the Oil Painting Phase

Palatable Choices: Shown above are tools for painting with artists' oils. For laying out and mixing colors I use disposable wax-coated paper palette sheets. The paints are squeezed from their tubes in small amounts along the edges of the palette and mixed in the center. For most color thinning and quick brush cleaning I prefer to use **Turpenoid** thinner. This odorless turpentine substitute can be bought in gallon tins and decanted into smaller, more convenient containers, such as baby food jars.

For mixing oils with metallic hobby enamels, use a hobby enamel thinner, such as **Humbrol** or **Testors**. These tend to "cut" better than Turpenoid. In any event, keep a separate bottle of thinner just for metallic paint mixes to avoid polluting your non-metallic colors with metallic flecks. *Note: if your hobby enamel thinner has a strong odor, keep the cap on the jar as much as possible and work in a well-ventilated area.*

The last "peas" to be added are, appropriately enough, medium-light green. Again, they have been applied in irregular clusters.

Discussion: If you have yet to paint a figure with a camouflaged uniform, this may appear to be quite an involved process. Certainly, there is more to "pea pattern" camouflage than there is to single-color uniform painting. But if you make regular checks against a good photo of the actual garment while you are painting, and give careful attention to the color balance, you will find that the camouflage scheme almost takes care of itself.

Still, it is inevitable that you will go back into the finished scheme to touch up a color or a shape here or there. This is not an unwelcome proposition; the additional variations brought about by touching up will add realism, because the original fabric designers permitted "errors" in their patterns to mimic the quirks of nature. The actual "pea pattern" camouflaged articles you are simulating were made using an artfully complex method of overlaying colors, much as is used with modern silk-screening.

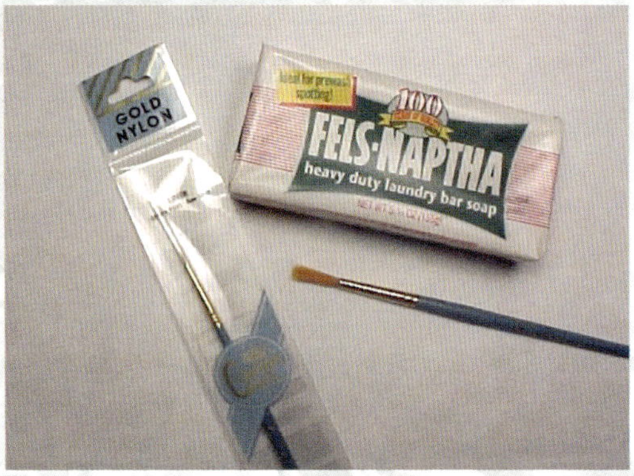

Wunderbar: It's not critical that you invest in expensive brushes for your painting. Even modestly-priced red sable or synthetic brushes will perform well, so long as they are properly maintained. A thorough cleaning after every work session extends each brush's life by preserving the shape and point of its bristles.

While attending art school I discovered **Fels-Naptha**, an inexpensive industrial-strength laundry soap that is sold by the cake. By gently rubbing the moistened brush tip into this soap *(right)* you can clean all the way through to the metal ferrule, preventing dried paint from accumulating and eventually ruining the brush's point.

Fine uniform details, such as the belt, buckle, decorations, cables, epaulettes, and divisional sleeve band have been painted in, completing the acrylic under-painting.
In the photo at right, the *obersturmführer* has already been treated with a deep initial oil glaze. The technique is discussed below.

Discussion: Features to highlight in this manner include: the upper bridge and tip of the nose; tops of the ears; a "catch-light" on the lower lip; some (but not all) of the knuckles of the hands; and the topmost areas of the hair. On the uniform, add touches to the upper edges of the lapels and the tops of clothing folds, taking care not to change the character of the camouflage pattern.
As you did with the Burnt Umber glaze, whisk these highlights with a soft, dry brush to blend them into the underlying paint. This will leave a remarkably subtle suggestion of scale lighting.
For highlighting those few colors that are lighter than human flesh tone, use Naples Yellow Light. Use a pure white highlight only when you are working on white garments and other articles.

A broad brush can be used for most blending work, but you may want to use smaller brushes to give particular care to the more delicate features.
Another advantage of oils is that they can easily be wiped clean from the figure, if your first attempts at blending are not to your liking.

Discussion: The first oil glaze simulates the shadows in the folds, creases, and undercuts on the figure. Using Burnt Umber mixed with a small amount of a deep blue or black, apply the glaze with a detail brush, working it not only into the smaller clothing folds and creases, but also onto broad areas of shadow. Such areas will generally include the armpits, crotch, sleeve openings, and in this instance, the back sides of the arms below the elbow, as well.
Next, using a slightly thicker glaze of the same color, carefully paint in stronger outline shadows along the lower contours of pronounced details, such as the badges, belt, lapels, and pocket flaps. The resulting effect will at first appear stark, but this will be corrected during the next step.
With a soft, dry brush about the size of the one shown above, lightly whisk the surface of the figure to gently blend (or "feather") the Burnt Umber oil glaze into the underlying acrylic colors. Here, the advantage of working with slow-drying oils will become obvious—the same subtlety can't be brought about as quickly and easily with fast-setting acrylics or hobby enamels. You will also find that the water-based acrylic undercoat holds up well under repeated oil paint glazes.

You can hasten the drying time of the Burnt Umber glaze by "baking" the figure in a light box for about twenty minutes (*see p. 31*). Once it has cooled, it will be ready to receive the first oil highlights. Use a fine brush and apply sparing highlights of Naples Yellow Deep oil color to those parts of the figure that would stand out in sunlight, irrespective of the underlying colors involved.

Spitting into the Wind: Once it has dried, treat the figure with a light dusting of Floquil Figure Flat. For my money, this is simply the most reliable matte finish available. It confers a dead-flat finish, eliminates distracting reflections in the areas of dried oil paint, and brings the colors into a kind of homogenous balance with each other.
Shake the can thoroughly to ensure an even spray, and spray out-of-doors if at all possible, as Floquil lacquer carries a noxious odor.

Afterglow: Not all of the *obersturmführer's* features will be left with a completely matte finish. On your own figures you will want to vary the lustre of certain items. This is easily achieved with acrylic clear coats, such as those available from Polly S.

Pure gloss finish is usually too reflective and garish for 1/35 scale figures. Satin finish (a roughly 1:1 ratio of gloss to matte) better imparts the "shiny" effect of polished boots, leather belts, metal buckles, and so on. Worn leather boots are effectively simulated by painting satin clear coat into the wrinkles and creases of the ankles and uppers while leaving the exposed portions (the points of likely wear) untouched.

Because it is not quite as flat as Floquil's Figure Flat, acrylic flat clear is usually enough to add a distinctive, dull glow to items, such as worn belts, shoes, and the unpolished metal of gun barrels.

The Finished *Oberstürmführer.*

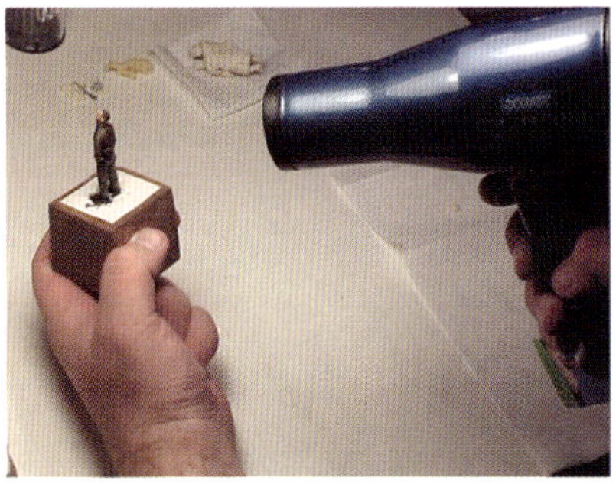

The aforementioned hair dryer, set on low heat, helps clear coats to dry evenly and quickly. It is also somewhat useful on oil glazes if you don't have a light box.

Finishing Figures with Acrylics and Oils: Considerations

(1) Choice of Acrylic Base Colors- As has been shown, the colors used in under-painting are critical, because they form the basis for the translucent oil glazing and top-coating to follow. Choose your acrylics by the appearance of the paint in the bottle rather than the label's description. You want pure, rich colors that will mix well—not washed-out tertiary tones that are marketed with claims of being specially developed for "scale accuracy."

(2) Acrylic Flow Improver- This inexpensive fluid slows drying time and improves coverage, facilitating both color blending and preliminary glazing during the under-coating process.

(3) Acrylics First- Although dried acrylic under-coats accept oil overlays well, the reverse is not the case. Only sparingly apply acrylics over an oil under-coat—preferably after sealing it with Floquil Figure Flat lacquer.

(4) Key Oil Colors- Following well-considered acrylic under-painting, the essential oil tones are Burnt Umber and Black for glazing shadows, and Naples Yellow Deep for simulating sun and top-lighting effects.

The *Obersturmührer* Takes His Place as the Gunner of the Zerstörer.

Picture Gallery: Modified 1/35 Scale Figures and their Terrain Bases

Presented here is an assortment of "panzer soldiers," all constructed, modified, and painted using the techniques discussed in this essay.

This *panzergrenadier* MG42 gunner halts along a path somewhere in Normandy. Both the figure and the base landscaping were finished as discussed in this essay.

The snow covering the rough Ardennes terrain beneath this *fallschirmjäger* is a dusting of **Hudson & Allen Studios'** Snow Powder. Touches of micro-fine glass beads add a shimmering effect.

A *panzer offizier* in walking-out dress, western front, 1944. Note the extensive insignia, painted with a mix of oils and silver hobby enamel. His shoes have been "polished" with a subdued Polly S. Satin and Flat Clear mixture.

To achieve a unified effect, the terrain base must be given the same degree of care and attention as the figure it frames.

Note the figure's hair, sculpted from epoxy putty as described in this essay.

The highlights to this tanker's hair were accomplished with the versatile Naples Yellow Light. Because of its warmth, it is usually a better choice than pure white.

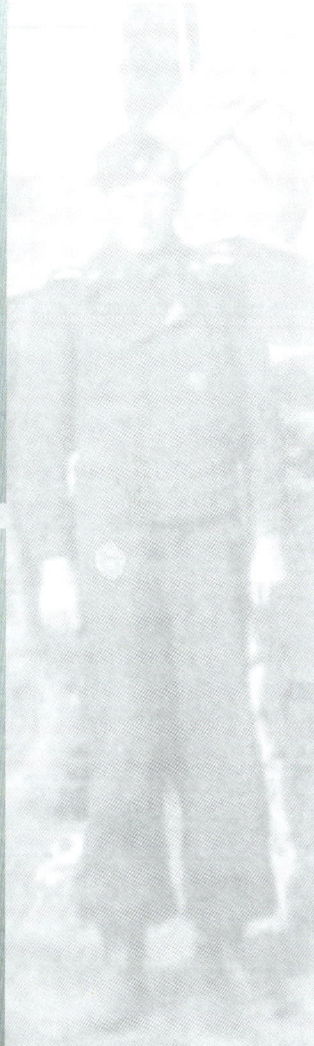

A NCO of the *Waffen-SS*, eastern front, autumn, 1943. His overcoat is a specially-tailored sheepskin garment. The submachinegun is an unusual model that was produced exclusively for the SS.

Note the flagstones, curbing, tree stump, blades of tall grass, and scattered leaves. These touches add interest and provide context. (Compare these camouflaged pants with those worn by the re-enactor on p. 35)

An assault gun crewman of the elite *Grossdeutschland* division displays his decorations, including a newly-awarded Iron Cross. Again, careful terrain treatment lends visual impact and breathes life into the figure. Here, the depiction of concrete rubble under this successful gunner is particularly apt: the chief role of the assault gun was to pulverize enemy strong points. The concrete's color is an example of one of the few instances when a pure white highlight is preferable to the warm tone of Naples Yellow Deep or Light.

– EFM

Panther Stellung

Bathos in Hitler's Bavarian Redoubt

IT IS SUMMER, 1945—HITLER'S "Great National Redoubt," Germany's last defensive bastion, the Alpine Fortress, does indeed exist.

As the Western Allies penetrate deep into the German homeland, the rumor of the existence of a vast Nazi stronghold to the south takes on greater and greater proportions. Some believe that Hitler, anticipating the capture of Berlin and other industrial centers to the north, has transplanted much of his military and economic might to a secret fortified area in Southern Germany, from where he plans to continue waging the war. Eisenhower finds the existence of this Great National Redoubt so plausible that he conducts his advance toward the Elbe River with a watchful eye upon his right flank.

And, somewhere in the forests south of Munich, a hilltop pillbox stands sentinel, one of many poised to repulse an enemy who must sooner or later come calling.

SS Stellung (armored strong-point) No. 28 is nothing more than a reconstituted Panther tank turret set into a concrete installation. On a limited scale, this innovation had seen service in Italy, where it met with some success defending vital stretches of road from similar hillside positions.

Men of the *Waffen-SS*, some of the last of Hitler's most committed and capable soldiers, occupy the Great National Redoubt. Their resolve is as formidable as the steel and concrete walls of the Stellung fortifications from which they will fight. Here, at No. 28, an *untersturmfuehrer* (non-commissioned officer) of SS panzer forces makes a leisurely orbit around his newly-rebuilt turret, touching it up with paint from a bucket. Although his steps are relaxed and his uniform is unkempt, this inveterate cigarette smoker is typical of the tough, seasoned defenders—few though they may be—who will figure so prominently in this, the final defense of the Third Reich.

Strictly speaking, this exotic panzer is not a panzer at all, but a portion of a classic panzer being put to an exotic use. It is a rebuilt Pz.Kpfw. V Panther turret in the role of a static anti-tank emplacement.

My inspiration for this project came from wartime photographs of similar emplacements in German-occupied Italy and in the suburban streets of end-of-war Berlin. However, I chose to place my Stellung in the hypothetical setting of the Great National Redoubt largely because it facilitated my long-standing plan to model an ambitious woodland terrain base. Hence, the Stellung finds itself in the forested hills of Southern Germany.

The 9" by 12" terrain base was designed to face forward on its shorter edge. A fairly steep slope begins its rise at the stream bed in the foreground, carrying the viewer across the hillside terrain features and up to the turret and soldier at the crest. From the tall, swaying grass punctuated with flower blossoms to the easy swagger of the panzer crewman figure, the overall composition is meant to convey a calm, pastoral atmosphere. The project essay that follows showcases some of the modeling techniques employed.

SS Stellung No. 28, Bayerischerwald, Bavarla, 1945.

Firepower in the Forest: This side view shows off the layout of the Stellung vignette to advantage. At right, the vignette's foreground is defined by a shallow, rocky stream. From this feature the ground rises sharply to meet with the rust-stained foundation of the Panther turret. By elevating the rear of this longitudinal vignette, the turret has been given a commanding position that compensates for its relatively small size. At the same time, the multi-level, "terraced" arrangement of the surrounding terrain features keeps them all readily accessible to the viewer.
Discussion: Viewers of dioramas and vignettes are drawn to natural features, such as elevations and watercourses. If you are developing your own composition but are uncertain about how to make it engaging, consider adding vertical elements, like a hill incline, or including a stream. These are generally good ways to begin.

The Big Build-up: After making a mock-up of the setting, I chose a 9" by 12" decoupage plaque to use for the scene. I glued 1/4" by 3" basswood strips around the edges to elevate the groundwork. These were first contoured with a scroll saw to match the intended roll of the terrain. Once assembled, the base was sprayed with **Krylon** Gloss Black paint. In this photo, styrofoam bits have been tacked in place to form a multi-level terrain foundation.
Before being glued in place, the wood block foundation for the turret was covered in **A+B** epoxy paste and stippled with a fine wire brush. Once dry, it was lightly sanded to impart a concrete texture.

Bore-Sighting: The planning stage. With its mantlet and gun barrel temporarily taped in place, the Panther turret has been set on its wood block foundation and fitted to the terrain base to establish a good compositional layout. Note that the block and gun barrel line up with the schematic penned onto the pinewood interior of the base.

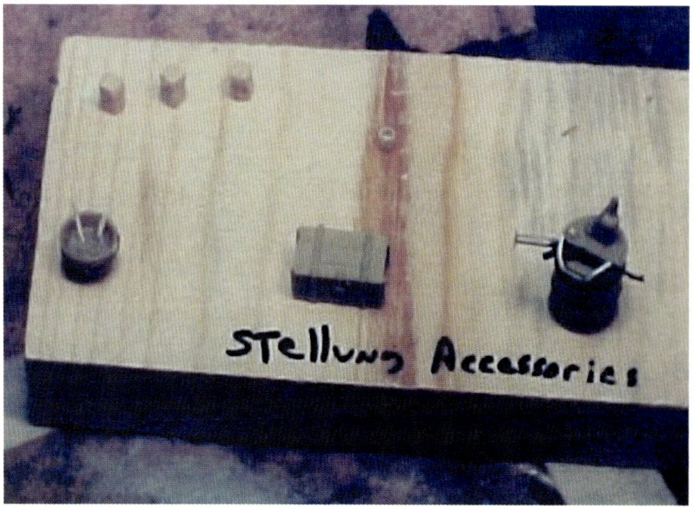

The Whole is Greater than Its Parts: Some of the accessories for the area behind the turret, white-glued to a wood scrap for painting. At left, the bucket has been filled with epoxy putty and two brush handles made from plastic rod. The fuel drum at right supports a frothing bottle of champagne and a sub-machine gun detailed with a lead foil strap and photo-etch strap buckle.

Site Improvement: While designing the stream bed feature I worked from pictures I had taken of creeks and rivulets near my home in Pennsylvania. In the photograph above, one such picture lays in front of the in-progress terrain base. These source pictures gave me good, representative details to simulate with dried roots, pebbles, and epoxy putty.

Discussion: Here, over the styrofoam I have added a thin layer of **Sculptamold**, an excellent papier-mache product. Note that the fine striations of the stream banks have already been sculpted from A+B epoxy putty and covered with dirt to add an earthen texture.

Epoxy putty is an excellent material for creating fine landscaping details. It dries more slowly than papier-mache, holds its form well during sculpting, and can be carved easily when dry. Epoxy putty also works well along the edges of the terrain base; unlike papier-mache, it forms a permanent bond that does not flake or curl away with time.

A Turret Among the Trees: The Stellung vignette begins to take its final form. The tree trunks, with their exposed roots, have been sculpted over the wooden dowel armatures. Tall grass from **Woodland Scenics** has been fixed in place with white glue. **Verlinden** "trees" flank the turret, which has been set in place for one last review of the composition. The turret will be painted separately from the terrain base.

Discussion: In many years of experimenting with terrain products, I have found no easy system for applying tall grass to 1/35 scale terrain bases. Some modelers drill mounting holes for it into their landscape material, but this leads to a sparse, regular effect that more resembles the rows of a hairbrush than patches of natural vegetation. It is better simply to take the time to apply the grass in clumps with white glue, working it into natural-looking patches with an old paintbrush as it sets in place. Adding diluted white glue during this process helps the grass to keep its form. Ironically, even after this, you have to trim the tall grass clumps carefully to give them an *uncut* appearance!

It bears noting now that I assembled the whole terrain base before painting it. While it might seem that it would have been easier to paint the various features individually before bringing them together on the base, there were good reasons for painting them all at once. All of the foliage was airbrushed with a black-green color to stiffen and strengthen the fragile trees and grass clumps, and to provide a deep underlying shadow effect for the colors to follow. Also, by having to handle only the display base while painting, I was able to keep from damaging these brittle terrain features.

Detail: The stream bed, underway. Dried roots and assorted pebbles have been positioned along the bed, which has been covered with a layer of dirt. Three wood dowels are visible on either side of the feature. These formed the bases of epoxy putty tree trunks, which were sculpted later.

Plastic Fantastic: The turret, from **Italeri's** Panther Ausf. A kit, in the process of being super-detailed. This top view shows most of the alterations to the basic kit.

I set out to model a turret rebuilt from the wreckage of a destroyed Panther tank. As such, the turret would combine features of both the early Ausf. D and later Ausf. A variants, reflecting that the repairmen used whatever parts were on hand.

Discussion: The pictures to follow highlight the changes I made to the Italeri turret. Note that every one of these changes was decided upon before assembly, in the planning phase; only then can you fully exercise your imagination and at the same time think through potential construction problems.

Starboard Side View: I wanted to make the damage on this reconstituted turret as obvious as possible, without having it appear unserviceable. The grey sheet plastic rhomboid on the corner of the side armor represents additional steel plate used to cover a shot hole.

Note that *zimmerit* (anti-magnetic mine paste) has been applied in a square pattern with epoxy putty. In the area of the shot damage, it has been blasted away, revealing a bare armor surface.

Left side detail, with interior of rear hatch.

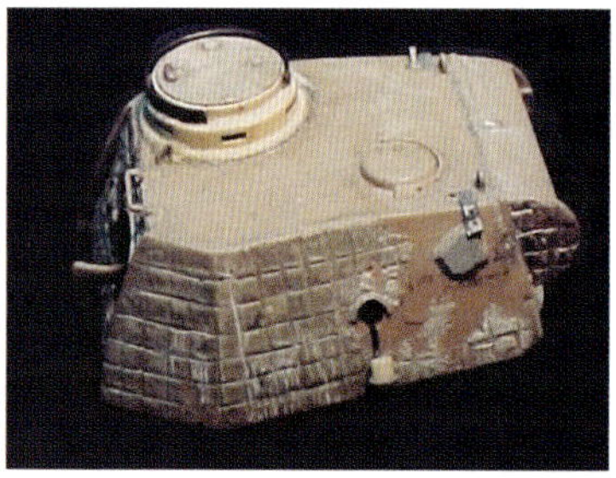

Potpourri: The styrene turret was detailed with many materials, including lead foil (smoke candle mounts), brass strip (cupola machine gun ring), ship model chain (pistol port plug), and wire (rear roof hand hold). The gun barrel is a fine turned aluminum accessory part by **Jordi Rubio**. Although it was not produced specifically for the Italeri kit, it fits the kit's gun mantlet quite well.

Epoxy putty was also used to create bolder weld seams, particularly along the turret roof where it joins the gun mantlet. As with the *zimmerit* coating, the putty was allowed to set in place, then textured with the back of a hobby knife blade.

Black Forest Cake: The base colors of the turret and foliage, applied by airbrush. I use **Tamiya** acrylic colors almost exclusively because of their rich, deep tones and compatibility with my airbrush.
The foliage has been sprayed with a deep green base color created by mixing I.J.N. Green with a little black. As already mentioned, this basic spray helped to stiffen and strengthen the foliage. It also established a "shadow layer" over which I would spray progressively lighter highlighting colors. This process of finishing terrain is time-consuming, but the results are worth it.

Watch that Attitude: The *unteroffizier's* body is an exceptionally fine resin offering from a company called **Blue Max**. Its sense of relaxed motion is extraordinarily life-like—a quality hard to find in stock figures in any scale. I exchanged the stock head for an appropriate **Hornet** replacement part, setting it at an angle to emphasize that the figure is examining his handiwork as he saunters around the turret. The cap, positioned to appear lazily seated on the *unteroffizier's* head, is a **Dragon** accessory, while the bucket is from Tamiya. Both the brushes and cigarette are plastic sprue, detailed with epoxy putty.
This solitary figure was intended to inject a strong but understated element of humanity into the vignette, thus imparting *bathos* to an otherwise exotic setting.

Painting the "Summer Oakleaf" Camouflage Pattern

In the second project essay, *A Soldier's Story*, I described my method for painting a typical late-war variant of the *Waffen-SS* "pea pattern" camouflage. Following is a similar method for depicting another late-war SS scheme, the one worn by the *unteroffizier* in this chapter: the "summer oakleaf" pattern.
Left: A modern-day re-enactor wearing trousers like those of the *unteroffizier*. Note the more predominant light green color.

The pattern is begun with an initial application of **Polly S.** #500829 Earth Red, followed by irregular patches of #501427 Ogre Dark Brown.* These patches vary in size and cover a little less than a third of the surface area.

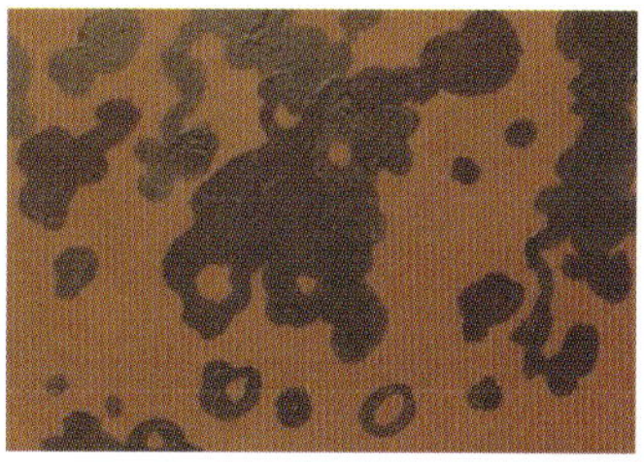

Next, Polly S. #505278, I.J.N. Green, is applied in a similar manner, but a little more sparingly than the Dark Brown. Note the occasional "ring" shapes. The I.J.N. Green covers about a quarter of the surface.

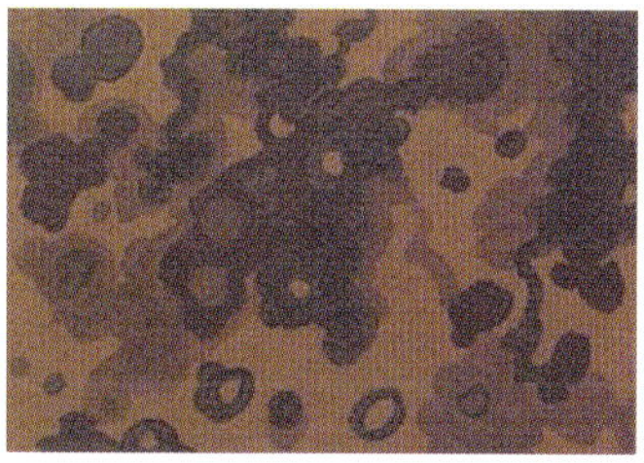

The third color, a 1:1 mixture of the Earth Red and Ogre Dark Brown, is added as shown. This touch of color simulates the "bleed" effect of the dyes in the actual garment. The basic Earth-Red color should still constitute about 50% of the pattern.

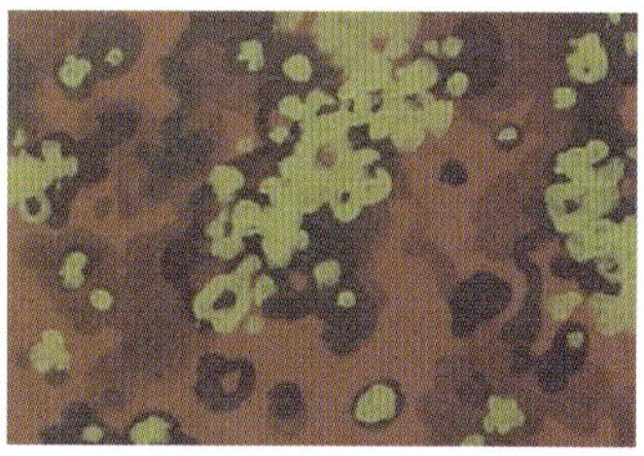

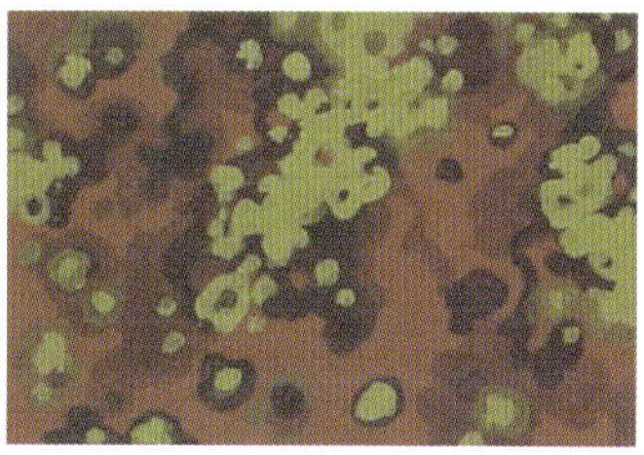

The last two stages show the application of the prominent color in the "summer oakleaf" scheme: a bright, distinct light green, mixed from Polly S. #501443 Carrion Light Green and #414278 Depot Buff in a ratio of about 3:2. Note how this is applied in intricate, variously-sized blotches.
In the last color panel, the light green mix has been darkened with I.J.N. Green and used to lay in occasional outlines around the light green patches to give the finished pattern the characteristic SS "silkscreen" look.

**Because of their particular usefulness with the colors in this scheme, I have identified the acrylic paints used by brand and color number in this second discussion of painting SS camouflage.*

The "Business End": The completed project, viewed down the awesome barrel of the Panther turret. Although the different types of foliage were first uniformly colored black-green to create an underlying shading effect, a broad range of terrain color highlights has been applied by airbrush to finish the various parts of the composition.

Discussion: Composing a vignette scene that is tight and full of impact is not exactly a science, but there are helpful guiding principles. In my view, good color balance and contrast are just as essential to the composition as is the physical arrangement of its parts.

With the Stellung, I have tried to pay tribute to the surprisingly broad tonal variations to be found in nature. At any time of year, woodlands exhibit a marvelous variety of colors. Even for subjects set in high summer, a full palette is available to the modeler who wishes to add depth to his landscape and emphasis to the terrain in his composition.

It should be noted that, regardless of the color of the terrain feature I was painting, my airbrushing method remained the same. I treated each feature to progressively lighter "dustings" of color, mixing down with a yellow or tan hue to simulate sunlight. (As a rule, I avoid lightening colors with pure white because it tends to result in a cold, chalky effect that is seldom convincing.) My technique was to limit the final highlights to the upper reaches of the tall grass and shrubs, creating a "top-lighting" effect.

A River Runs Through It: A bird's eye view of the finished stream bed. *Center:* note the assortment of rocks and pebbles along its course, as well as the damp tree roots emerging from the earth of the upper bank. Even a mere trickle of a stream makes a compelling impression upon the viewer. Here, the water was modeled by painting the flat areas of the bed with a deep mud color, then varnishing with Tamiya Clear Gloss.

The shaggy grass along the stream banks was highlighted by hand to place further emphasis upon the transition between forest floor and muddy rivulet.

Note how some areas of the earthen stream banks carry a blanket of moss. I simulated this by impressing Woodland Scenics ground foam into patches of the epoxy putty landscaping material before it had cured. Subtle green tones mixed in with a glazing technique during the final terrain painting completed the effect.

Stumped: Apart from adding color, a wooden wire-post with a printed notice, blooming flowers, and the base of a recently-felled tree also contribute to the "story" behind the vignette. The notice suggests that the vicinity is off-limits; the flowers convey the season of the year; and the stump, surrounded by fine sawdust, shows that a field of fire has been cleared for the turret.

The stream bank, viewed from the turret.

Creature Comforts: The stretch of bare, earthen forest floor behind the turret serves as the platform for a paint bucket, drop cloths, jerry cans, ammunition pouches, and helmets for the Stellung's crew.

The "paint" in the bucket is the standard Dark Yellow formula, which after spring of 1943 became a basic German vehicle camouflage color. Note the ribbons of paint running down from the brim of the bucket—a small detail that contributes to the impression that work is even now in progress. The Dark Yellow is being used by the *unteroffizier* to touch up the turret. The helmets, in keeping with an occasional late-war practice, were issued in the same color.

The drop cloth at left is stained with the Primer Red paint used to undercoat panzers.

Rust Never Sleeps: Instead, it forms wherever bare metal comes in contact with moisture, then washes down with each new rain, staining porous surfaces like the concrete foundation of the Stellung.

Discussion: These rust streaks were painted in with an oil glaze. The color tones I use combine Burnt Sienna and Burnt Umber, in varying proportions. Acrylic colors can also be employed for glazing like this, but artists' oils give a deeper, richer effect.

Note the less pronounced rust effects on the turret side, particularly around the welded armor patch in the corner abutting the mantlet.

Detail: Rust has also crept into the nooks and crannies of the turret roof. This much rust might seem excessive if found on a "working" tank; not so with this old turret.

Guns and Liquor: The submachinegun, fuel barrel, and bottle of champagne rest in the shade at the edge of the woods. A small ammunition box sits in the foreground. At right, note the contents of the bucket being carried by the *unteroffizier*: the same red primer as mentioned above.

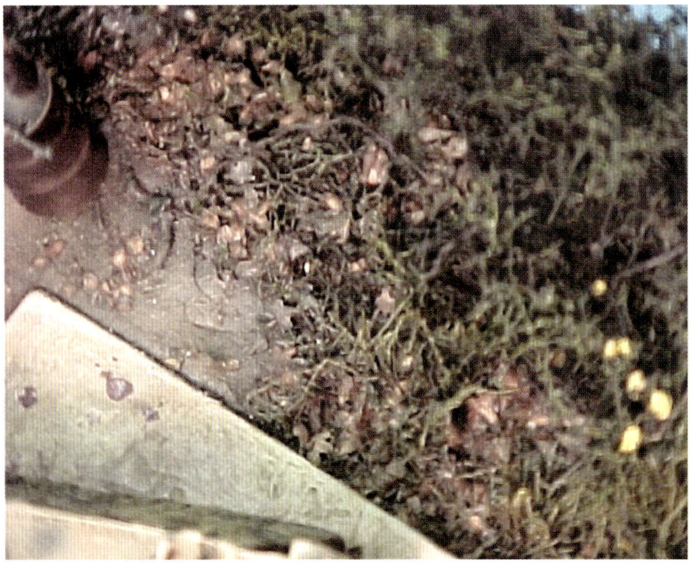

Grass and weeds surround the concrete foundation.

Forest Litter: Even in the middle of summer, the floor of a typical forest is home to decaying leaves and other debris from the previous autumn. For the modeler, simulating this brownish litter is a way to inject contrast and color variety into a terrain base that might otherwise appear too uniformly green.

Hudson & Allen Studios offers a broad variety of terrain accessories, including excellent autumn leaves. I scattered some around the bases of the bushes on either side of the Stellung turret. Although they come in an appropriate brown color, I glazed mine with acrylic paints to put them in harmony with the rest of the landscape.

Botanical Blandishments: Flowers have been placed in a number of locations across the vignette's landscape. For these I used a type of dried flower from a craft store—the kind with clusters of small, bulbous tips called "Galaxy Gyp."

In the picture at top, Galaxy Gyp has been used to fashion Snapdragons and Dandelions; at bottom, a grouping of the same flower with longer stems stands slightly higher to represent Buttercups.

Dried flowers are extremely brittle and therefore very hard to paint by hand. It is better to use an airbrush to under-paint them first, taking care not to allow the force of the air to damage the stems. The blossom color is then deposited in droplets, not brushed on.

Panther Stellung, Burning Bright: This photo gives a good overview of the terrain effects previously discussed. Note the dark brown tone of the stream bed, the medium green tones of the short grass, and the deep greens of the tall weeds and shrubs on either side of the turret. The flowers, forest litter, and freshly-cut tree trunks provide strategically-placed color contrasts.

-EFM

Commander, Stellung No. 28:
This *unteroffizier* wears a black panzer jacket, a non-regulation sweater and late-pattern "summer oakleaf" tanker's trousers. Note the gray metal tank assault and Nazi Party badges (both in profile, left breast); the special gold embroidered *SS* arm eagle (left bicep); the pink piping of the panzer forces on his early-pattern Field Gray soft-peaked officer's cap and shoulder strap trim; and lastly, an unusual variation of the *3rd SS Panzer (Totenkopf)* divisional cuff band: here, an "officer's death's head," which was sometimes seen on the arms of long-serving veterans of that division.

The Horror of Yugoslavia

A Dark Moment During the Struggle for the Balkans

IT IS SUMMER, 1942—THE BLOOD-BATH THAT WAS THE war in the Balkan states is in full swing. Internecine bickering has been going on here in Bosnia, Croatia, and Serbia since the Middle Ages, when Western European powers decided to arm the peoples of this mountainous region and create a buffer state against the Ottoman Empire. Now, the Balkan conflict takes on a new dimension, as one of the most murderous sideshows of the Nazi sweep against its enemies in the east. The arrival of the Germans has added aggravation to an already aggravated situation. Chetnik (royalist) and partisan (communist) forces have been antagonizing each other for years; the new Nazi presence only fans the flames. As a local saying goes, "there's a gun in the attic of every farmhouse here." And the warring factions of the Balkans are as intolerant of the Germans as they have always been of each other.

War is not fought according to rules here. Long-standing hatreds run deep and find expression in atrocities throughout the occupied areas. Blood is on the hands of almost all of the belligerents. The Germans police the forest roads, fall victim to ambushes, and then order reprisals. Executions follow, and the vicious cycle continues.

Here, in the form of a vignette, I have tried to give expression to aspects of the tragedy of the guerrilla conflict that was fought in the Balkan states (i.e., the former Yugoslavia) during the Second World War. The composition consists of three components: a mass grave to advance the premise; a pair of supporting figures to define the circumstances; and a captured French Char B 1 (bis) heavy tank to act as an additional supporting element, helping to frame the scene.

This Char was confiscated by the Germans after their earlier victory in France. It has been impressed into police service with the Seventh SS Mountain Division *Prinz Eugen*, a formation which spent the bulk of the war as an anti-partisan unit in Yugoslavia. The tank overlooks a fresh, lime-covered mass grave of murdered partisans. Despite its imposing size, the Char stands as a secondary vignette element. It is a panzer grey monolith, a mute, brooding witness to the enormity in the ditch that stretches across its path.

By contrast, two SS soldiers in the foreground pass by the Char as they stroll toward the grave, their noses covered with kerchiefs. They appear to be engaged in casual conversation; in light of the circumstances, their callous nonchalance borders on the obscene.

I began this project with certain concerns. From conception I intended for it to be disturbing and thought provoking, but worried that it might end up looking revolting. So I proceeded with an awareness that the final result must achieve an appropriately balanced commentary, both graphically and morally. The critical consideration was, of course, the mass grave. This feature is drawn from numerous accounts of the early-war killings committed by the Nazi *einsatzgruppen* ("special action groups"). These murders were comparatively unsystematic, and this fact allowed me to draw details from a number of sources without having to incorporate the most explicit aspects of any one. Thus, the atrocity takes the form of a pit containing bodies covered with tarpaulins and sprinkled with lime powder. Blood and gore are in this way kept to a minimum, and the lime powder evokes an appropriately ghostly atmosphere. I hope you will agree that this approach helped to successfully convey the grim reality of the Balkan conflict without resorting to unnecessarily graphic details.

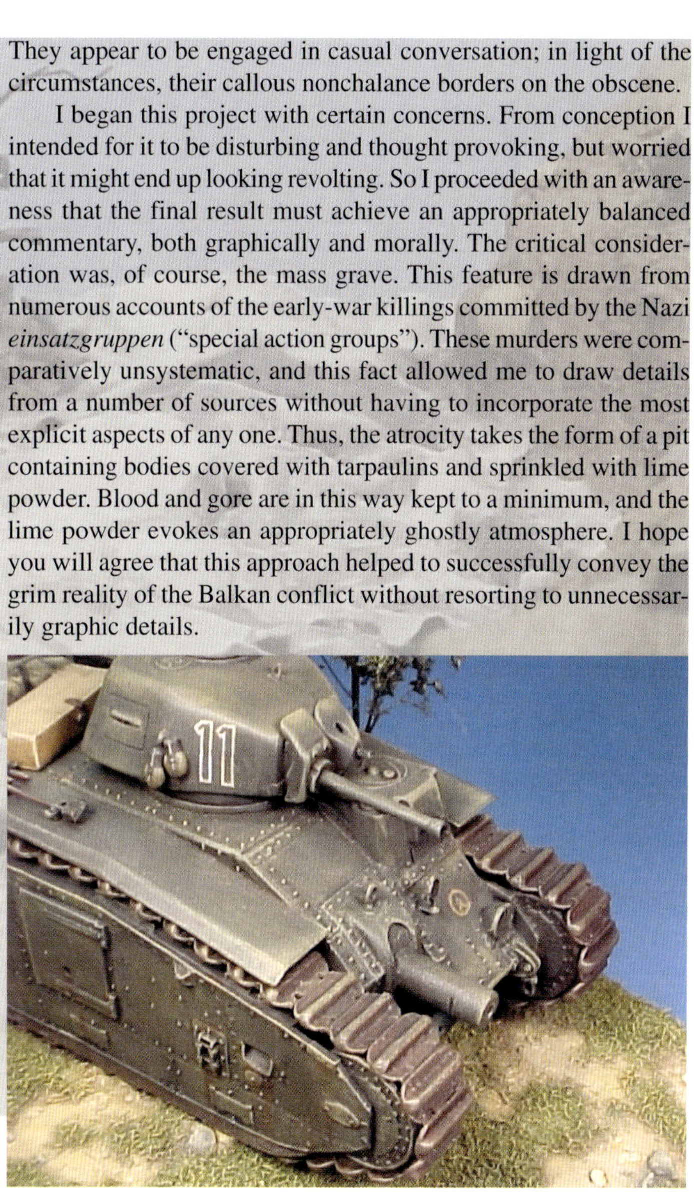

Char Extraordinaire: This excellent resin kit by Al-by of France has been finished in Panzer Grey.

Vanilla Fudge: The Char B 1(bis) is a fine kit from the French manufacturer **Al-by**. Before anything else, I assembled it to the point shown in these photographs. Once it was together, I used both its horizontal and vertical dimensions to decide upon the length, width, and height of the terrain base.

The Char, which was one of the best tanks fielded by the French just before the war, has been a subject long awaited by armor model enthusiasts. Although not available in 1/35 scale styrene plastic as of this writing, Al-by's resin version is a pleasure to build. While expensive, it isn't nearly as tricky as many other resin offerings.

Full Kit: Photographs of French tanks as they appeared before their capture by the Germans in 1940 are fairly uncommon, but enough exist to illustrate how they were equipped by their original owners. Generally, the French did not stow much gear on the exteriors of their Char B tanks, beyond certain essentials, such as heavy tow chains and a few tools. However, the Germans tended to stow equipment and supplies on their tanks liberally. Hence, the wealth of gear on the rear deck of this Char.

Discussion: Placing exterior equipment has to be undertaken thoughtfully—especially when dealing with unusual vehicles relegated to unusual roles. I tried to balance my desire to incorporate as much detail as possible against the question, "what would a German crew have stowed on a captured French tank being used to support second-line police formations in a war against partisans?"

Details, Details: While experimenting with the placement of various accessories, I searched for a spot for this delicately molded resin box. Ultimately, I left it off; the Char's new owners would not have allowed it to hamper the turret traverse, as it would have done here.

Roadside Assistance: I included a photo-etch detailed German medium tank jack and wood block on the hunch that they might have been useful with the Char. Months after completing this project, I came across documentary film footage of the actual French jack, being used by the French before the German invasion. It was quite different in appearance and operation, and this put me in doubt about whether the German jack could have been used on the Char.

Discussion: A lack of necessary documentation at the time a project is being built sometimes inspires the armor modeler to take leaps of faith. As often as not, information turns up later that appears to undermine those leaps. When it does, don't write off your project as no longer valid; no one can claim to be consistently accurate. Go ahead and make those leaps of faith.

And, to the best of my knowledge, the question of whether the German jack would have been useless with the Char remains unanswered.

Char Noir: Once completely assembled, including external stowage, the Char was thoroughly cleaned with **Polly S.** Plastic Prep, then sprayed with several light coats of **Floquil** Primer Black. A lacquer-based primer like this works well for sealing "multimedia" kits (i.e., those composed of many materials, such as resin, plastic, and brass) for further painting.

Balkan Bravoes: The SS soldiers in this vignette come from the excellent **Hornet** line of figures. Although they are marketed individually, they work so well together that I can't help but think they may have been designed to complement each other, as they do here. On the figure at right, I replaced the stock head with one from Hornet's line of accessory heads, choosing a bald head so that I could later sculpt in the figure's hair with epoxy putty.

Discussion: White metal figures are heavier than the more common styrene plastic and resin ones, and can pose a challenge when it comes to securely mounting them to painting and display bases. A solution similar to the one described in *A Soldier's Story* (*p. 32*) is shown in the picture: attach a sheet plastic shim to the block with white glue before drilling the figure mounting hole, then insert and affix the figure's brass stem with cyanoacrylate glue. The bond holds sufficiently during the painting process, but upon the figure's completion it can easily be dissolved with the help of acetone, or by carefully working a hobby knife blade under the heel to "crack" the foot free.

One of the completed figures, with epoxy putty hair added.

First Impressions are Lasting: The terrain base, with carefully positioned grave pit, was constructed as described in the project essay dealing with the Panther Stellung turret vignette (*p. 43*). Again, the assembled Char was used to help determine the base's final dimensions. To create an effect of weightiness, the tank and the two lime drums were pressed into the wet **Sculptamold** terrain material. With their positions on the base established, I removed these components before the groundwork dried. At the same time, I pressed the Char's treads into the earth behind it to simulate ground torn up in its wake.
This process not only added realism to the overall scene, but also established convenient location markers for repositioning the tank and accessories after the terrain had been painted.
In the above photo, the Sculptamold has already set, and static grass has been glued in irregular patches to represent dry, parched summer turf.

Tank Topography: This overhead view of the nearly completed terrain shows how the grave pit was scalloped into the contour of the base's front and rear edges.

The Victims: an epoxy putty foundation has been laid in the pit, and two castings of corpses have been embedded. The additional limbs were taken from my spare parts box and modified to suit the scene.

The Devil's Handiwork: The Nazi *einsatzgruppen* executioners sometimes covered their victims' bodies before spreading lime powder over the grave and filling it in with earth. To simulate tarpaulins, I covered most of the forms in the pit with facial tissue, fixing it in place with diluted white glue. This photo shows the tissue after it had been painted a deep greenish grey. Note the several flesh-toned human heads and hands emerging from the covering—hopefully, just enough humanity revealed to express the point intended.

Anonymity in Death: The subtle suggestion of a proposition often has a greater impact than does an overt statement about it. Thus, covered in tarpaulins and dusted with lime powder (baking soda), the victims of the pit are not immediately recognizable for who they are. Assuming the forms of indistinct apparitions, they demand fairly close inspection before the viewer grasps the enormity of the scene.
I would like to think that the approach I took towards modeling these fallen partisans resulted in an appropriately stark portrayal of the subject, one which is at the same time sensitive to human dignity.

Thematic Reinforcement: A large spade hangs over the mass grave from the opposite earthen bank, on the edge of the vignette. This is a part from the old **Historex** line of Napoleonic accessories in 54 mm, a slightly larger scale than the 1/35 of the Al-by Char and Hornet figures. The scale discrepancy did not trouble me, because I was specifically looking for a large shovel that would be easily noticed.

In its chosen location, the spade serves several purposes. It adds a counterbalancing vertical element to the far right side of the composition, an area of the base that is otherwise flat. The spade also strengthens the premise of the mass grave, and implies that a pile of earth rests nearby, waiting to be shoveled back into the pit.

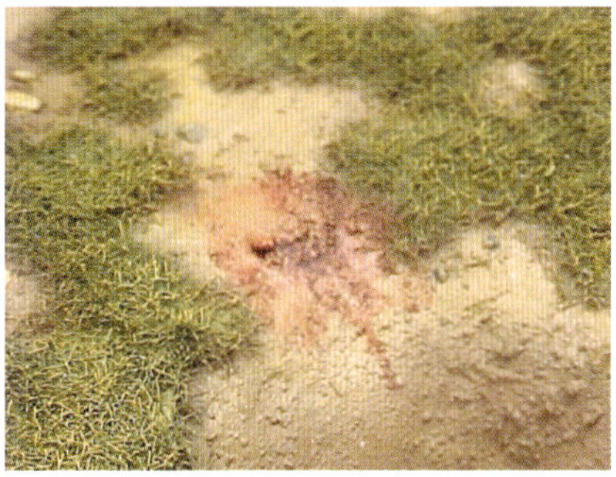

The Murder Scene: The only explicit portrayal of blood in the vignette is found at a single spot along the edge of the pit. It marks the place where each partisan was gunned down, then allowed to fall one by one into the waiting grave.

Instruments of Crime: Nearby, barrels containing the lime powder and another shovel furnish additional circumstantial evidence of recent violence.

Mountain Greenery: I constructed this small tree using the methods described in the project essay dealing with the Panther Stellung. The natural beauty of the Balkan countryside is particularly evident in the warmer months, when it fills out with rich green foliage. This tree was shaped into a lean, tapering spindle to resemble a cypress, which is common to the region.

The Char B 1 (bis) holds vigil as *Waffen-SS* soldiers approach the mass grave.

Tool boxes, jerry cans, a bedroll, and other equipment reside upon the rear deck of the Char B 1 (bis).

Somber Grey Sentinel: Although much of the foreign equipment impressed into German service is said to have been left in its original color scheme, the forces of occupation have repainted this new police vehicle in Panzer Grey, a color that was commonly used on second-line vehicles throughout the war. Following my references, I gave the Char double-digit turret numbers, and in several places marked it with the *Prinz Eugen* divisional emblem.

Discussion: As already seen, the painting of the Char started with a primer coat of Floquil Primer Black, which works well as a foundation shadow color on subjects that will have deep final finishes. I first airbrushed with **Tamiya** German Grey, then applied progressively denser highlights to select areas to emphasize shadows. To lighten, I mixed in small amounts of Tamiya Sand, concluding the process with a final acrylic highlight to contours and edges using a Polly S. stone color.

Creating highlights over grey tones is particularly problematical. Simply mixing down with white paint leads to an unnaturally cold, chalky finish. On the other hand, mixing a warmer sand tone into the highlight helps to create a subtle impression of sunlight and faded paint without markedly altering the grey hue, and gives a finish that ties in with dusty groundwork. However, the sand tone must not contain too much yellow, or the final result may have more of a greenish cast than intended.

War Paint: The standard German *Balkankreuz* and the *Prinz Eugen* divisional emblem adorn the left side of the Char.

Standard Equipment: The original French heavy tow chain has followed the Char into Balkan service. I can't help but wonder how useful a conventional link chain like this would have been in recovering a heavy tank like the Char. Still, so many wartime photos show them slung upon these tanks that it was almost a given that I should include one in this vignette.

As with all tank accessories, I chose to paint and weather this metal chain. I began with a deep acrylic brown color, then glazed with Burnt Sienna and Burnt Umber oil tones to create a rusted effect. **Testors** silver enamel tinted with a touch of Burnt Sienna served as a final highlight. The same treatment was given to the tracks.

Rare Earth: I wanted the vignette's groundwork to have the quality of packed, sun-baked soil with intermittent patches of dry grass. To this end, I made sure to apply the Sculptamold terrain material smoothly in those areas where packed earth would show through.
Clusters of rocks were embedded in the wet Sculptamold to add interest to certain areas. These were a combination of street gutter stones and plaster shards, painted in greys and browns to mirror the color variety found in nature.

Enduring the Elements: Unlike that found on most contemporary tanks, the Char's running gear was covered by large, flat armor plates. The fine detail of the rivets, seams, and various hatches on the plates of the Al-by kit simply cried out for weathering effects.
Rust was applied in vertical streaks and patches using diluted Burnt Sienna oil paint, with Burnt Umber mixed in to vary the hue. The dust and dirt effects were brought about with varying concentrations of Naples Yellow, dry-brushed and feathered. I applied it sparingly, working it into the armor plating for a subtle dust effect, then topping off with straight opaque Naples Yellow highlights to the top edges of the access doors, hinges, and rivets. Lastly, Ivory Black mixed with a little Burnt Umber was laid in to add definition to seams and recesses, and applied to appropriate spots to simulate grease and grime.
All the vehicle markings began as decals. As we have seen, these have a filmy quality that often resists even a flat varnishing spray, so after these were applied I painted over them in matching acrylic colors to achieve a uniform finish.

Don't Tread on Me: The Char was a vehicle of substantial size. I tried to underscore this by modeling a "wake" of deep track marks behind it to help indicate its weight.
Discussion: Note the difference in tone between the dark, damp sod of the track runs and the much lighter expanses of dusty, dry ground. Attention to details such as these makes for surprisingly realistic effects at a minimal cost in additional time or effort. As in other art forms, the last embellishments made to your project are the first to be experienced by the viewer, so it pays to give thought to finishing touches.

Masked Bandits: To strengthen the thematic connection between the mass grave and the SS men, I sculpted kerchiefs from **Duro** epoxy putty onto their faces. These masks look to be a sanitary precaution, but they are also intended to sustain an impression of criminality.

For the purpose of this vignette, it is not particularly important whether these soldiers were personally involved in the executions of the partisans in the mass grave. Rather, I intended for them to symbolize the *einsatzgruppen* and similar criminal organizations, and therefore to underscore their collective responsibility for the innumerable atrocities they committed.

In the shadow of the Char, the two policemen of the Nazi occupation stroll indifferently towards the final resting place of the murdered partisans. The centuries-long tragedy of brutal war in the Balkans continues.

–*EFM*

An Exotic Panzer in Action:
Some time in 1946, a Krupp/Steyr 8.8 cm Pak 43 weapons carrier attached to the *1st SS Panzerkorps* participates in a combined-arms raid against U.S. forces in Czechoslovakia from its base in the crumbling Reich's Alpine Redoubt.
This prototypical vehicle carries a brush-dappled "ambush" camouflage scheme, applied using leftover stocks of armor dark yellow and *Luftwaffe schwarzgrun* (black-green) paint.

Geheim

"Alles Kaput"

Tragedy and Desperate Improvisation as the Third Reich Crumbles

IT IS MAY, 1945—THE BATTLE FOR Berlin—the final battle of the European war—a struggle fraught with ironies, paradoxes, and contradictions. Near the Brandenburg Gate, ardent, even fanatical Nazi troops and their acolytes soldier on in the face of certain annihilation, protracting the city's suffering for the simple sake of war itself. Several blocks away, weary realists throw down their guns and surrender, or run for the asylum they hope to find among the Western Allies. Some city residents seek safety by isolating themselves in cellars; others, particularly the elderly, bravely dodge the unceasing barrages of artillery to favor a neighbor with a charitable act. A mélange of defeated souls, all lifelong Berliners, watch their ancient city crumble under the remorseless pounding of rockets. From some of their shattered windows, the response is incredulity; from others, only oblivious stares.

At great risk, many of the healthier denizens persist in their daily routines, only to belatedly grasp that these rituals no longer hold meaning. Schoolboys "play chicken" with low-flying Soviet fighter planes; closer to the front lines, teenage Hitler Youth cower in their foxholes, paralyzed by fear.

With the uneasy calm following the fall of Berlin, the smoke clears away, revealing myriad absurdities. In the zoo, the corpse of a hippopotamus reposes in its pool, impaled by an unexploded mortar shell. Nearby, an orangutan chatters merrily, its human caretaker picking his way across a plateau of bodies to bring over its noontime meal. Outside, more death: a Russian officer oversees the execution of an unruly subordinate; to either side, lamp posts strung with the innocent victims of the Nazis' own "flying courts-martial" bear silent witness.

And everywhere are children, the next generation of Berliners, their senses overwhelmed by the presence of death, their world collapsed around them.

Alles Kaput, a vignette measuring only six by eight inches, was conceived to put across in an encapsulated manner the desolate atmosphere just after the fall of Berlin. I entered into this project with a tight, lavishly-detailed composition in mind. I also intended it to be a subtle balancing act between "living" and inanimate elements.

The vehicle, a Borgward demolition tractor mounting a hastily-improvised recoilless gun assembly, has only lately been impressed into service by a few of the city's stalwart defenders. Although it occupies the center of the composition, it is not positioned to dominate the scene. Rather, it acts more as a focal point for the various "events" of the vignette. These include the body of a young woman, which is respectfully shrouded beneath a Persian carpet and placed "in state" on top of the Borgward; two soldiers, each from a different branch of the German ground forces, despondently awaiting their fates at the hands of their approaching captors; and in the background, gentle interaction between a vivid red cardinal, perched on a street sign, and a curious kitten. These oblivious little creatures betray what so many of Berlin's survivors were to come to observe: that spring was in the air, and that life's irrepressible cycle renews itself—even in the sepia-tinted squalor of a city which for all practical purposes appears to have just died.

The pictures that follow showcase the most noteworthy features of *Alles Kaput*. I hope that these photographs will inspire those miniature artists who have yet to attempt modeling urban ruins. The accompanying captions are intended to highlight the relevant modeling techniques.

"Alles Kaput": Literally, "Everything is Finished."

The Raw Materials of the Project: Reference sources, after-market accessories, decals, and my own notes surround a mock-up of the vignette. While it is sensible to enter into every project with a detailed plan, I always allow for in-progress additions and changes.

Discussion: The Borgward kit is by **ADV/Azimut**, a French company renowned for its clean castings and fine detail. Here, I have placed the tiny vehicle's upper hull on the **Verlinden Productions'** plaster street corner display base to get an impression of how the finished vignette will appear. Although I was not immediately settled upon the arrangement, a fresh look a day or so later left me satisfied. I felt that the display base made just enough of the desired suggestion of a bombed-out urban area without overpowering the diminutive Borgward.

Many modelers cultivate methods that make the process of assembly an orderly and comfortable one. For me, there's no better juncture at which to begin employing good habits than at the very beginning—from the moment an idea comes to mind and makes its way onto a notepad.

A Borgward, a Building, and a Bird: This compact composition is intended to balance man, machine, and urban ruin. Note that the attention to detail has been consistent—no one element overshadows the others.

Where the Work Begins: My work space for assembling and detailing (but not painting) the *Alles Kaput* project components. I use zip-lock bags to separate the various kit parts by category, such as basic vehicle parts, detail parts, diorama on-ground items, etc. This helps to keep the work table organized, and minimizes the chances of misplacing the smaller pieces. As the reader will see, my work area tends to become at least a little bit cluttered!

A Tractor with Some Teeth: The initial phase of converting the Borgward from a demolition vehicle to a self-propelled gun. The recoilless rifle, a separate resin kit from **Mini Art Studios**, is permanently attached. The muffler, situated below the gun shield, has been treated with Primer Red paint and dusted with baking soda to simulate corrosion. This treatment has been carried down to the lower hull, as well.

Well Into Assembly: The Borgward, now fitted with many of its small details, as well as the kit's white metal track links. As a rule, I assemble as much of the kit as possible before beginning to paint it. *Upper Right:* The road wheels have been test-fitted against the terrain base's contours. With their final positions established, they have been glued in place. The "sprung" suspension effect created by this wheel arrangement gives even the little Borgward a weighty appearance.
Discussion: Two-part epoxy glue is the adhesive of choice for a resin assembly requiring strong joints, as with these wheels. Another advantage of epoxy is its slow setting time, which allows time for positioning parts properly. Because the parts of many resin AFV kits lack positioning pins, this second advantage of epoxy glue is especially valuable.

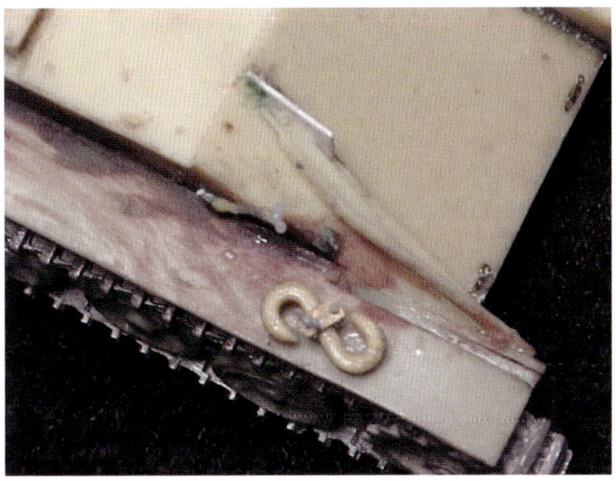

Hull-top Detail: The "S"-shaped towing clevis is secured by a brass plate and **Grandt Line** bolt and wingnut. Primer Red has been applied to the fender joint to confirm that the fender and hull connection is clean.

The *Mise-en-Scene:* At every stage of the vignette's development, the constituent elements were brought together and examined.
Discussion: I worked on the terrain base even while completing the vehicle. Early in the construction, I decided to extend the Verlinden base's dimensions at the front and right side, sculpting additional cobblestones with **A+B** epoxy putty. (At the same time I added loose bricks, other plaster debris, and a photo-etch manhole cover.) Content with the new proportions, I went on to complete the base's details.
Although few modelers seem to employ it in terrain base construction, A+B putty is an excellent landscaping compound. It can be sculpted into delicate features, such as the cobblestones of a European town street, or simply used along the outer edge of papier-mache bases, where it makes for a strong and permanent bond with the underlying base wood.

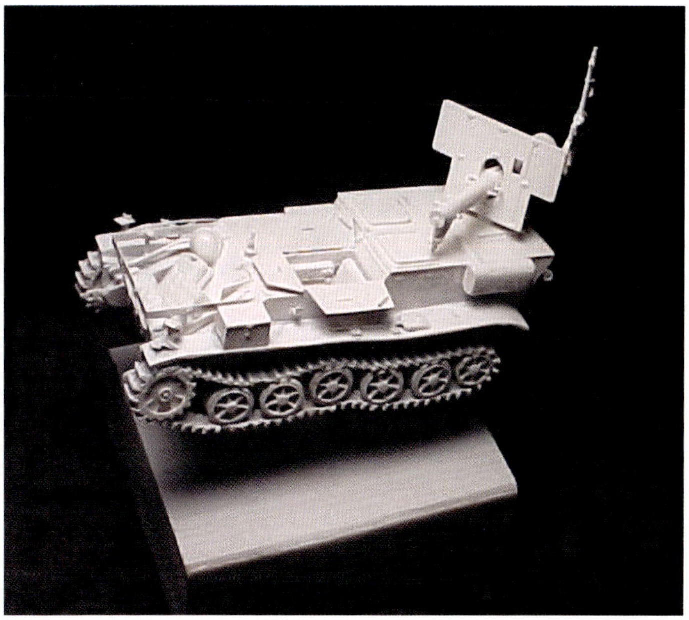

Prime Borgward: The completed gun carriage, under-painted with **Floquil** primer spray, then followed with a brush to the hard-to-reach areas. The scrap metal frame on the front was made from brass strips and wire.

True Colors: The Borgward has been given its basic colors—**Tamiya** Dark Yellow for the chassis, German Grey for the gun.
Discussion: Note that a jerry can, box, helmet, and tent roll have already been fixed in place in the bow frame. I find it easier to paint many detail items after attachment; with these particular details, attachment after painting was not an option anyway. The tent roll was made from tissue paper coated with thinned white glue, so the articles lodged above it had to be impressed into the roll while it was still wet to give them the impression of weight.

The Damaged Lamp: Early on, I missed the fact that I had left the "panes" completely intact!

There Goes the Neighborhood: The vignette display base, in progress. The predominant colors are acrylic brick red and concrete grey. To add richness and depth, the base was glazed with Burnt Umber artist's oil paint.
Discussion: At left can be seen the finished lamp, hanging from its electrical wire on the corner of the building. After I first assembled the lamp *(preceding picture)*, it dawned on me how unlikely it would have been for the glass panes to have survived the same blasts as have virtually razed the building. Rather than start over, I looked for an explanation for including the intact lamp, but found none that was plausible.
Like myself, most modelers are inclined to rationalize an error or oversight before correcting it. This tendency should always be resisted. Otherwise, you talk yourself into living with a project that is only a partial success, and the compromised feature remains disturbingly evident to you, if to no one else. On the other hand, nipping the problem in the bud as soon as you detect it preserves your sense of control over the project and adds to your confidence.

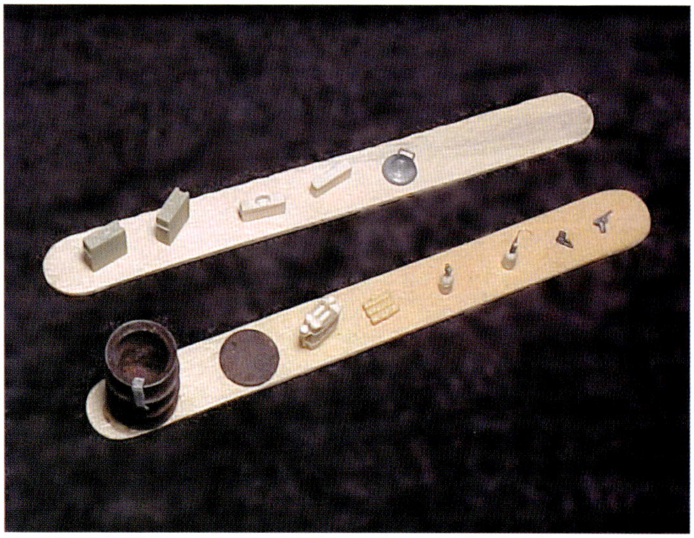

Base Accessories: Set up for individual painting.

Bringing Up the Rear: Although it does not line up feature for feature, my Borgward demolition tractor was based upon photographs of an actual vehicle captured by U.S. forces. Much of the battle damage visible on the model was directly inspired by damage found in those photographs, and in others. Sometimes the most realistic (and consequently, convincing) battle damage relates to missing rather than bent or broken parts and assemblies. For example, at lower left on the rear plate of this vehicle there is a tangle of twisted metal and wires where once there was a convoy light.
Discussion: On the same surface, note the appearance of paint flaking around the spots of bare, rusted metal. Here, the paint is not actually flaking away; the flaking has been simulated with what I call a *tromp l'oeuil* ("trick of the eye") effect. During the weathering process, deep reddish-brown "rust spots" were painted onto the plate. After this, the peeling "paint flakes" were added by painting in dramatically lighter spots of the base camouflage colors on the areas bordering the rust spots. Two principles are key to successfully bringing about this effect. First, you have to be selective about where you paint the flakes, because completely encircling the underlying rust spots does not look realistic. Second, actual peeling paint seems to flake in a regular, almost linear, manner. Therefore, the more or less random technique that we usually employ when weathering AFVs is not helpful here. Instead, try basing your work on examples from real life. AFVs on display at ordnance museums, caterpillar tractors at roadside excavation sites, and even old automobiles are all useful sources.

Curbside Armory: A burnt, rusty old barrel serves as the centerpiece in a cluster of guns, Panzerfaust anti-tank weapons, ammunition belts, Molotov cocktails, and mines. The subdued metallic finish of the barrel was accomplished by painting with a mixture of silver hobby enamel and artist's oil colors.

The rubble and jetsam of war

Supporting Cast: Three human forms flank the Borgward—two soldiers and the body of a young woman.

A Signpost Avian and a Frolicsome Feline: The cardinal began life as a songbird from Tamiya's Livestock Set. I modified it with epoxy putty tail feathers and placed it atop the ruined street sign. Below, a curious Siamese kitten reaches for the red bird. This little survivor was for me a crash course in sculpting animals. I patterned him after a picture found on a bag of cat food at the supermarket, and extrapolated his form with details culled from a book about cats. Correctly sizing this epoxy kitten was a challenge—not only because of the novelty of the subject, but also because I had to walk a fine line in making him neither imposingly large nor unnoticeably small.

Peddler's Paradise: The bow of the Borgward was designed to hold a wedge-shaped demolition charge, which was to be driven to its target and deposited by either a human operator or by remote control. This Borgward, however, has been fitted with a scrap metal basket to hold ammunition for its field-fitted recoilless gun. Now, after most of its ammo has been expended and the crew anticipates its capture, the basket of the vehicle serves only as a repository for salvage.

The basket items are a mix of military and civilian articles, and were selected to help recreate the atmosphere of whimsy and absurdity that has been noted in photos and reports of the last days of the battle. Among the strange array are a marble bust, *á la Rodin*; a bucket; a stringed musical instrument; water bottles; and helmets.

An Improvised Gun Deck: This photograph shows to advantage the extensive weathering performed on the Borgward. Again, the *tromp l'oeuil* effect of flaking paint can be seen on the top plate. The gun shield betrays a heavy coating of grime and rust streaks, both simulated with controlled oil paint glazes and washes. The bare metal tread plate below the breech was not part of the Borgward kit, but a spare part that I added to represent a field-modified gunner's step. The anti-aircraft machine gun and the sighting chart to the right of it likewise are add-on parts. A camouflage-pattern field cap rests on the hull corner.

The Handwriting on the Wall: In many German cities towards the end, personal messages chalked on the bombed-out walls of ruined dwellings proliferated. Typically, a message verified that its writer was alive and inquired of the whereabouts of lost family members. Anyone who knew something about the persons mentioned in the message could chalk in a response.

The message of *Alles Kaput* reads "Where is Ms. Lieslötte Schaller? -R. 7/4/45 (April 7, 1945)."

Perhaps the body of Ms. Lieslötte Schaller reposes just a few feet away, on the deck of the Borgward...

The chalked writing was added to the interior of the Verlinden ruin with a light grey **Prismacolor** pencil.

Sinkhole Season: The water in this small shell-hole serves both to add interest to the vignette and to speak to the squalid conditions in Berlin at the close of hostilities.

Partially submerged bricks and a porcelain plate help to highlight the translucent quality of the pool, which was made with a small amount of epoxy resin colored with a brownish-green enamel hobby paint.

A Small Arsenal for Surrender: A pistol, stick grenades, and boxes of ammunition have been placed in front of the Borgward in anticipation of surrender. The defeated soldiers hope that this forthcoming gesture will encourage fair treatment from their captors.

Above: Note the stick grenade wired to the fuel can to create a makeshift incendiary bomb. In the desperate last days of Berlin, anything went if it gave the defenders some firepower or bought them a little more time.

An Appeal for Peace: The surrender flag was made from epoxy putty. I rolled it out flat, let it set for about forty minutes, then sculpted it to shape. Gentle heating in the light box accelerated the curing process and preserved the flag's shape.

Leopards and their Spots: The soldier in the black jacket *(top)* came from a Tamiya figure set, but saw several modifications. The head was replaced with one from Verlinden that had a suitably haggard and dejected facial expression. I added **Duro** epoxy putty hair, running it down into the eyes in the manner so typically seen in photos of German prisoners of war. The trousers were painted in the "summer oakleaf" camouflage pattern of the German *Waffen-SS* forces (the technique employed is described on p. 47).
The blond soldier *(bottom)* wears a jacket made from Wehrmacht "splinter camouflage" cloth, noteworthy for its larger and sharper patches of color.

Tragic Element: The body of the young woman was formed from a **Friulmodellismo** mannequin and epoxy putty. The Persian carpet covering her was photographed from a book, reduced to scale size, and printed on ink-jet printer paper. I was concerned that the ink might bleed if I shaped the rug with diluted white glue, so instead I just carefully wrapped it around the body, securing it at several points with cyano-acrylate glue.

The Borgward vignette, from the front right corner.

Epilogue: "Everything is finished." This photo shows to good effect the subtle ways the two survivors are displaying dejected moods. Note that the front of the gun shield has also been weathered with oil color glazes, and that the gun tube has been capped shut. Clearly, the Borgward's war career has drawn to a close.

The cardboard ration box under the barrel *(center right)* is a card stock accessory from **Hudson & Allen Studios**. The box folds together like the real article. I added wrinkles to mine to give it a dinged appearance, and applied earthen stains with acrylic colors to put it in character with the rest of the vignette.

Discussion: This last harmonizing touch may seem trivial, but it makes a vast difference in the end. I have seen countless AFV models on display at conventions and in hobby shops, all carefully finished, and each one almost spoiled by distracting features, such as bare thread tie-down ropes, gaudy railroad lens headlights, or unpainted pewter chains wrapped around the bow. Most model builders agree that unpainted plastic is unsightly and unrealistic; not as many seem to concur about the appearance of unfinished non-plastic parts on their models. Perhaps there is a temptation to use them as-is because they are often made of the same stuff as their real-life counterparts. In my view, it takes very little—sometimes just a quick oil glaze, or a touch of flat clear paint—to turn these eyesores into attractive and convincing details.

– EFM

A Street Corner Named Destruction: Roof tiles, cables, and shattered glass lay atop the pile of rubble at the base of the ruined building. The glass shards, which can be seen in the area right under the ruined lamp, were fashioned from broken pieces of clear styrene. I carefully placed them with tweezers, then coated them with a clear satin finish. Without this coating, these garish plastic bits would have been much too shiny to be representative of dusty pieces of glass.

Afterword

HOPEFULLY, THE PROJECT ESSAYS OF THIS BOOK HAVE fulfilled their purpose: to introduce armor modelers at all levels of accomplishment to the fascinating world of the lesser-known and hypothetical German fighting vehicles of World War Two, the exotic panzers. Throughout this volume I have shared a number of modeling techniques that have served me well during many hours of work, and over many years of dedication to this wonderful genre. If this book has inspired you in your own panzer projects, exotic or otherwise, then it has done its job.

Admittedly, these pages chronicle some ambitious modeling efforts. Certainly, it has not been my plan to discourage you from attempting your own exotic panzer by creating an impression that extraordinary investments in time, money, or effort must be made. The projects I have covered in this book began with fairly expensive resin kits and conversions, and the decision to take each one as far as I did was as much a matter of personal taste as it was a reflection of my commitment to the art form.

But these are the best of times for all armor modelers, whatever individual budgets may allow. These days, brand new styrene kits appear on hobby store shelves and mail order lists almost weekly, and many of these are not only exotic, but are sharply priced and easily assembled as well.

Only limitations of space and subject matter considerations precluded me from covering styrene models in general. However, the leading styrene manufacturers have done so much in recent years to advance our art form that an enthusiastic endorsement is in order. Many thanks to **AFV Club**, **Dragon**, **Italeri**, **Tamiya**, and others too numerous to name here. Your excellent kits continue to fix new armor modeling horizons for all of us.

And my thanks to you, fellow panzer model enthusiast, for your attention and interest. I hope our mutual pursuit brings you much satisfaction for many years to come.

A Bicycle Built for Two . . . Panzerfausts: Perhaps the ultimate exotic panzer would be the most unlikely—an anti-tank rocket bicycle piloted by an aging *Volkssturm* conscript, Berlin, April 1945.

About the Artist

Edward F. McGrane was born in Havertown, Pennsylvania, in 1963. He graduated from Tyler School of Art (Temple University) with a Baccalaureate in Fine Art, Painting, in 1984. His fascination with the German Panzers began at age ten with the advent of Monogram Models' Panzer IV series of tank kits. A dedicated miniaturist, his interests run the gamut from armor and aircraft to scale figures, and he is an accomplished sculptor and painter of both historical and surreal subjects. Although he has exhibited and sold paintings in galleries, his first loves are the historical miniature figure and the armor diorama. With a mind towards promoting the scale model as a bona fide art form, Ed has displayed at major regional and national figure shows for years, where his miniatures consistently generate excitement and dialogue among fellow armor enthusiasts.

Notes